HISTORICAL RESEARCH IN
EDUCATIONAL SETTINGS

DOING QUALITATIVE RESEARCH IN EDUCATIONAL SETTINGS

Series Editor: Pat Sikes

The aim of this series is to provide a range of high quality introductory research methods texts. Each volume focuses, critically, on one particular methodology enabling a detailed yet accessible discussion. All of the contributing authors are established researchers with substantial, practical experience. While every book has its own unique style, each discusses the historical background of the approach, epistemological issues and appropriate uses. They then go on to describe the operationalization of the approach in educational settings drawing upon specific and vivid examples from the authors' own work. The intention is that readers should come away with a level of understanding that enables them to feel sufficiently confident to undertake their own research as well as to critically evaluate other accounts of research using the approach.

Published and forthcoming titles

Michael Bassey: *Case Study Research in Educational Settings*
Morwenna Griffiths: *Educational Research for Social Justice*
Gary McCulloch and William Richardson: *Historical Research in Educational Settings*
Jenny Ozga: *Policy Research in Educational Settings*
Christopher Pole and Marlene Morrison: *Ethnography in Educational Settings*

HISTORICAL RESEARCH IN EDUCATIONAL SETTINGS

Gary McCulloch and William Richardson

Open University Press
Buckingham · Philadelphia

Open University Press
Celtic Court
22 Ballmoor
Buckingham
MK18 1XW

email: enquiries@openup.co.uk
world wide web: www.openup.co.uk

and
325 Chestnut Street
Philadelphia, PA 19106, USA

First Published 2000

A catalogue record of this book is available from the British Library

ISBN   0 335 20254 3 (pb)   0 335 20255 1 (hb)

Library of Congress Cataloging-in-Publication Data
McCulloch, Gary,
    Historical research in educational settings/Gary McCulloch and William Richardson.
        p.   cm. – (Doing qualitative research in educational settings)
    Includes bibliographical references and index.
    ISBN 0-335-20255-1 – ISBN 0-335-20254-3 (pbk.)
    1. Education–History–Research–Methodology.   I. McCulloch, Gary.
    II. Richardson, William, 1956–   III. Title.   IV. Series.
LA21.M33 2001
370′.7′2–dc21   00-036726

Typeset by Type Study, Scarborough
Printed in Great Britain by St Edmundsbury Press Ltd, Bury St Edmunds, Suffolk

Contents

List of figures

List of case studies

Series editor's preface

I had never realized just how fascinating research was in its own right. I was expecting the research methods course to be boring, difficult and all about statistics but I couldn't have been more wrong. There is so much to consider, so many aspects, so many ways of finding out what's going on, and not just one way of representing it too. I have been really surprised.

(Student taking an MA in Educational Studies)

I never knew that there was so much to research. I thought that you just chose a method, applied it, did your statistical sums and came up with your findings. The reality is more complicated but so much more interesting and meaningful.

(Student taking an MA in Educational Studies)

The best thing for me was being told that qualitative research is 'proper' research – providing it's done properly of course. What goes on in schools is so complex and involves so many different perspectives that I think you often need a qualitative approach to begin to get some idea of what's going on.

(Student taking an MA in Sociology)

I really appreciate hearing about other researchers' experiences of doing research. It was quite a revelation when I first became aware that things don't always go as smoothly as some written accounts seem to suggest. It's really reassuring to hear honest reports: they alert you to pitfalls and problems and things that you might not have thought about.

(Doctoral student)

Comments such as these will be familiar to anyone who has ever taught or taken a course which aims to introduce the range of research approaches available to social scientists in general and those working in educational settings in particular.

The central message that they convey seems to be that the influence of the positivist scientist paradigm is both strong and pervasive, shaping expectations of what constitutes 'proper', 'valid' and 'worthwhile' research. What Barry Troyna wrote in 1994, continues to be the case; namely that:

There is a view which is already entrenched and circulating widely in the populist circles . . . that qualitative research is subjective, value-laden and, therefore, unscientific and invalid, in contrast to quantitative research, which meets the criteria of being objective, value-free, scientific and therefore valid.

(1994: 9)

Within academic and research circles though, where the development of post-modernist and post-structuralist ideas have affected both thinking and research practice, it can be easy to forget what the popular perspective is. This is because, in these communities, qualitative researchers from the range of theoretical standpoints utilize a variety of methods, approaches, strategies and techniques in the full confidence that their work is rigorous, legitimate and totally justifiable as research. And the process of peer review serves to confirm that confidence.

Recently, however, for those concerned with and involved in research in educational settings, and especially for those engaged in educational research, it seems that the positivist model, using experimental, scientific, quantitative methods, is definitely in the ascendancy once again. Those of us working in England and Wales go into the new millennium with the government endorsed exhortation to produce evidence-based research that,

(firstly) demonstrates conclusively that if teachers change their practice from x to y there will be significant and enduring improvement in teaching and learning; and (secondly) has developed an effective method of convincing teachers of the benefits of, and means to, changing from x to y.

(Hargreaves 1996: 5)

If it is to realize its commendable aims of school effectiveness and school improvement research, as portrayed here, demands 'objectivity', experiments and statistical proofs. There is a problem with this requirement though and the essence of it is that educational institutions and the individuals who are involved in and with them are a heterogeneous bunch with different attributes, abilities, aptitudes, aims, values, perspectives, needs and so on. Furthermore, these institutions and individuals are located within complex social contexts with all the implications and influences that this entails. On its own, research whose findings can be expressed in mathematical terms is unlikely to be sophisticated enough to sufficiently accommodate and account for the myriad differences that are involved. As one group of prominent educational researchers has noted:

We will argue that schooling does have its troubles. However, we maintain that the analysis of the nature and location of these troubles by
the school effectiveness research literature, and in turn those writing
Department for Employment and Education policy off the back of this
research, is oversimplified, misleading and thereby educationally and
politically dangerous (notwithstanding claims of honourable intent).

(Slee *et al.* 1998: 1–9)

There is a need for rigorous research which does not ignore, but rather
addresses, the complexity of the various aspects of schools and schooling:
for research which explores and takes account of different objective experiences and subjective perspectives, and which acknowledges that qualitative
information is essential, both in its own right and also in order to make full
and proper use of quantitative indicators. The *Doing Qualitative Research
in Educational Settings* series of books is based on this fundamental belief.
Thus the overall aims of the series are: to illustrate the potential that particular qualitative approaches have for research in educational settings; and
to consider some of the practicalities involved and issues that are raised
when doing qualitative research so that readers will feel equipped to embark
on research of their own.

At this point it is worth noting that qualitative research is difficult to
define as it means different things at different times and in different contexts.
Having said this, Denzin and Lincoln's (1994) generic definition offers a
useful starting point:

Qualitative research is multimethod in focus, involving an interpretive,
naturalistic approach to its subject matter. This means that qualitative
researchers study things in their natural settings, attempting to make
sense of, or interpret, phenomena in terms of the meanings people bring
to them. Qualitative research involves the studied use and collection of
a variety of empirical materials . . . that describe routine and problematic moments and meanings in individuals' lives. Accordingly, qualitative researchers deploy a wide range of interconnected methods,
hoping always to get a better fix on the subject matter at hand.

(Denzin and Lincoln 1994: 2)

The authors contributing to the series are established, well-known
researchers with a wealth of experience on which to draw and all make use
of specific and vivid examples from their own and others' work. A consequence of this use of examples is the way in which each writer conveys a
sense of research being an intensely satisfying and enjoyable activity, in spite
of the specific difficulties that are sometimes encountered.

Whilst they differ in terms of structure and layout each book deals with:

• The historical background of the approach: how it developed; examples
of its use; implications for its use at the present time.

- Epistemological issues: the nature of the data produced; the roles of the researcher and the researched.
- Appropriate uses: in what research contexts and for which research questions is the approach most appropriate; where might the research be inappropriate or unlikely to yield the best data.

They then describe it and discuss using the approach in educational settings, looking at such matters as:

- How to do it: designing and setting up the research; planning and preparation; negotiating access; likely problems; technical details; recording of data.
- Ethical considerations: the roles of and the relationship between the researcher and the researched; ownership of data; issues of honesty.
- Data analysis.
- Presentation of findings: issues to do with writing up and presenting findings.

Over the past few decades, research into the history of education has gone out of fashion. Whereas, in the 1960s and into the 1970s, the majority of all initial teacher education courses involved some study of the history of education, there no longer appears to be any space – or any need – for such work to be undertaken. Partly as a consequence, but also arising out of other trends and developments, there are relatively few educational historians working in institutions of higher education and history of education is not a heavily populated research field. Nor is there much in the way of literature to encourage or to guide those who may wish to venture therein.

Gary McCulloch and William Richardson's book, *Historical Research in Educational Settings*, makes an eloquent, and timely, restatement of the potential importance of historical research in education and education in historical research. Perhaps it is inevitable that education and schooling are always changing and being changed in the attempt to better meet the changing and various needs of society. On the basis of the view that history is a social necessity, that history is to society what memory is to the individual, some awareness of what has gone before and explanations as to why things might be as they are, would surely seem to be of great value. Clichéd though it might sound, we reject the lessons of history at our peril. Given that many current 'innovations' in policy and practice have their historical doppelgangers, this seems particularly pertinent.

Historical Research in Educational Settings is comprehensive, scholarly and practical. The authors write for educationists and social scientists new to historical research and for historians new to educational topics. They invite all readers to recognize, acknowledge and question their (discipline-based?) assumptions and prejudices, not least by the way in which they present historical research in education as a controversial and contested domain.

For anyone who is considering embarking on historical research for the first time, there is practical advice on locating, using and analysing evidence. The book makes much use of examples to illustrate processes, problems and opportunities.

As series editor of the *Doing Qualitative Research in Educational Settings* series I was always very keen to include a text on historical research in education. Gary McCulloch and William Richardson have made an original contribution to a disgracefully neglected area.

Final note

It was Barry Troyna who initially came up with the idea for this series. Although his publishing career was extensive, Barry had never been a series editor and, in his inimitable way, was very keen to become one. Whilst he was probably best known for his work in the field of 'race', Barry was getting increasingly interested in issues to do with methodology when he became ill with the cancer which was eventually to kill him. It was during the months of his illness that he and I drew up a proposal and approached potential authors. All of us knew that it was very likely that he would not live to see the series in print but he was adamant that it should go ahead, nonetheless. The series is, therefore, something of a memorial to him and royalties from it will be going to the Radiotherapy Unit at the Walsgrave Hospital in Coventry.

Pat Sikes

References

Denzin, N. and Lincoln, Y. (1994) Introduction: entering the field of qualitative research, in N. Denzin and Y. Lincoln (eds) *Handbook of Qualitative Research*. California: Sage.

Hargreaves, D. (1996) Teaching as a research-based profession: possibilities and prospects. Teacher Training Agency Annual Lecture. London: TTA.

Slee, R. and Weiner, G. with Tomlinson, S. (eds) (1998) Introduction: school effectiveness for whom?, in *School Effectiveness for Whom? Challenges to the School Effectiveness and School Improvement Movements*. London: Falmer.

Troyna, B. (1994) Blind faith? Empowerment and educational research, *International Studies in the Sociology of Education*, 4(1): 3–24.

Acknowledgements

We should like to thank everyone who has helped us to write this book. David Crook, Joyce Goodman, Allyson Holbrook, Roy Lowe, Tom O'Donoghue and Guy Whitmarsh were kind enough to comment on an advanced draft of the manuscript. Our colleagues and students at the University of Sheffield have been a continual source of ideas. The research networks and societies in which we have been involved have also contributed greatly to this study, in particular the History of Education society (UK), the American History of Education Society, the Australian and New Zealand History of Education Society, the British Educational Research Association, the American Educational Research Association and the Royal Historical Society. Our roles as editor and reviews editor of the international journal *History of Education* have also helped to enhance our understanding of the theory and practice of this field of research, and our appreciation of those who work in it.

We are grateful to Taylor & Francis Ltd, 11 New Fetter Lane, London, EC4P 4EE, for permission to reproduce a figure that originally appeared in *History of Education*, Vol. 8(3), p. 237.

May we also take this opportunity to thank Shona Mullen at Open University Press for her commitment to this project, and the series editor, Pat Sikes, for her equally enthusiastic support.

A glossary of key terms used in the book appears on pages 130–1; please note that each of these terms is highlighted in bold type where they first arise in the text.

We of course accept full responsibility for all errors of fact or interpretation.

1 | Getting started

This book explores the application of historical research to the field of education. Given the mountain of historical research that was devoted to education across the English-speaking world during the twentieth century it is curious that, to the best of our knowledge, only two previous volumes on this theme have appeared in English, the first over half a century ago, the second more recently but at a very introductory level. In writing the first detailed appraisal of modern times we have considered at length the form and content which might serve as the most useful introduction to the field. The form finally adopted reflects our concern to write for both the novice researcher and the more seasoned campaigner, bearing in mind also that the researcher experienced in education may be new to history and, similarly, that those experienced in history may be new to education. The content of the book engages with contemporary debates about historical research, locates historical research in education in its various academic settings and offers pragmatic guidance to those entering the field.

At the same time, we have tried to avoid duplication of a burgeoning literature on the theory and practice of history, social research and educational enquiry. Many of the best of such texts are easily accessible in libraries and we are content merely to point readers in their direction. Instead, our intention has been to explore the opportunities and difficulties presented by a field that sits sometimes uneasily at the intersection of these three traditions. To do this we have considered it essential to tackle both the theoretical and practical questions that arise. But before we get to grips with this task in detail the remainder of this chapter sets the scene in three short sections. The first covers our aims, purposes and scope; the second provides guidance as to how to use this book; the third asks the reader to begin 'thinking historically'.

Aims, purposes and scope

In this book we have two main aims. The first is to offer practical advice for researchers who are new to historical research in education, and are considering what kinds of possibilities it may hold for them. With these readers in mind we have set out to provide a broad introduction to research in this area, with a general emphasis on Anglo-American literature supported by British case studies, but also with a wider international and comparative dimension across the English-speaking world, including Australasia. We intend that the book should embody a source of information and advice as well as offering an early staging post for researchers who may wish to undertake detailed historical study. It provides a map of the field together with a compass for directions.

At the same time, we have thought it necessary to undertake a review of continuing controversies in the field, how these have been debated and exemplified in the work of established and prominent authorities and the pitfalls they imply for the unwary. As already noted, there have been very few full-length studies on this theme. Brickman's American survey (1949, reprinted 1973 and 1982) is now over 50 years old and completely outdated. Brickman was 'concerned with the application of the historical method to concrete examples and problems in the field of education', and his book provided the student of that era with a wide range of 'specific instances of how historiographical procedures may be used in historical research' (Brickman 1949: iv). In contrast, Petersen (1992) eschewed historiography in his short and practical 'handbook' to the field since, in his experience, 'an excess of theory has been found to bring on a paralysis of the creative impulses' (p. 6). Instead, his slim volume serves as a useful introduction to Australian sources. We know of no other comparable works that deal with educational **historiography** in depth, and it is especially striking that no previous attempt has been made in the British context. There is nevertheless a useful volume that brings together major statements on the study of the history of education by leading English practitioners during the twentieth century in order to document the 'making of the discipline' (Gordon and Szreter 1989), while Aldrich's *An Introduction to the History of Education* (1982) provides a short account of the main events in the history of education in England rather than a historiographical analysis.

A volume such as this is therefore clearly long overdue. While focusing principally upon the distinctive issues relating to historical research in education, we will seek to engage also with related types of research, especially in the social sciences. In pursuing this aim, we will highlight comparisons and contrasts with these other areas that can deepen an understanding of historical method. Thus, we explore ways in which historical research has been employed in a complementary and integrated fashion, alongside other research traditions, as well as in a separate and independent manner. As a result, we hope that this book will be a stimulus to both researchers in the English-speaking world who are interested in historical perspectives and methodologies as their sole or main approach to educational enquiry, and those who are attempting to combine these with other forms of educational research. As well as providing a map of the territory, we seek to establish contiguities with neighbouring states, and the subsidiarity and interdependence that these involve.

These primary goals are ambitious in themselves, especially given the broad scope of historical research relating to education, the diverse nature of work in this field and the rapidity of change in approaches to it over the past generation. Nevertheless, this book also sets itself some further, related objectives. First, it seeks to provide a restatement of the potential importance of historical research in education and education in historical research, while at the same time identifying pressures that especially over the past decade have tended to obscure and often to marginalize it in educational studies. In this respect it is important for all those entering the field, be they beginners or established authors, to recognize and acknowledge deeply ingrained assumptions and distinctive concerns that, internationally, have often differentiated the academic study of 'history' and 'education'. Such distinctions are reflected and reinforced in institutional arrangements in higher education, especially in the different character, aims and constituencies of history departments and education departments in Britain, North America, Australasia and elsewhere. No less significant are fundamental debates that have arisen in these countries, especially during the 1990s, over the character of historical and educational research. In locating the book within this broader context we hope to provide not only a map and compass, but also a survival kit designed for threatening and often hostile conditions.

In approaching these tasks, we seek to work not towards closure but towards open and continuing cultural debate. This involves approaching historical research in education as essentially a controversial and contested field, rather than as a consensual endeavour. Even so, we also hope to suggest ways of bridging many of the methodological disputes that have kept 'education' and 'history' at arm's length. The skills and insights usually associated with historical research are important assets when addressing educational issues, just as the experiences of educational theorists and practitioners can be valuable for **historians** researching education. Research in this area has attempted, not altogether successfully, to appeal to both kinds of work, historical and educational. To lose sight of the contribution that each can make in a common endeavour may be to diminish both. Therefore, a key set of issues that this current work raises, and that we will attempt to answer, is how far historical research in educational settings can satisfy both historical and educational criteria; whether it can achieve this simultaneously; and, if so, how.

Our exploration will draw principally upon an established field of study generally known as 'history of education'. This field had a recognizable identity throughout the twentieth century, and its role, while often contested, was at least until recently widely appreciated as being significant, especially among educationists. In the British case, for example, the leading educational historian W. H. G. Armytage could note in the 1950s how books on the history of education were tending to 'exfoliate', and that the subject had become 'not only an integral part of the training course [for teachers], but a field in which a great deal of research is being done by teachers themselves' (Armytage 1953: 114). In the 1960s, another major contributor to the field, Brian Simon, insisted that 'There is no need to make out a case for the study of the history of education as an essential aspect of the course offered to intending teachers. It has long been accepted as such in most colleges and universities and is almost universally taught, in its own right, as part of the education course' (Simon 1966: 91). Indeed, in the late 1960s and early 1970s there was a great deal of interest and new research in the history of education, not only on the part of educationists but also among academic historians in England and internationally (Richardson 1999a), with a great deal of interesting and important research resulting. However, the history of education has become less fashionable as a research field in the English-speaking world than it was in the 1970s, and its institutional base, especially in university education departments, has been severely eroded. In these circumstances it is especially important to review developments in the field, to reappraise the key methods and issues involved and to take stock for the future. It is no less crucial to highlight the challenges that this area continues to pose for a wide range of researchers, whether they are based in educational studies, or in history, or in any of the social sciences.

How to use this book

Given the approach just outlined, it will be clear that we are addressing the present book to a potentially broad and diverse audience. Three main kinds of reader may be identified:

- researchers principally concerned with the advancement of education and interested in how to incorporate an historical dimension within this aim;
- those with experience or training in historical method who seek insight into how to relate this to the study of education;
- those with a social science background, whether broad or based on a specific social science discipline, who require advice on how to develop both their historical awareness and their sensitivity to educational issues.

Within these groupings may be those embarking on their first research project – for example, the dissertation requirement of a postgraduate degree – alongside more experienced researchers new to this field of study. Finally there will be many researchers working outside the United Kingdom who will wish to compare our analysis with their own experience and national context.

Providing a single, accessible and relatively brief text to satisfy each of these audiences is a difficult task. Nevertheless, we believe it to be a necessary one, in view of both the absence of other treatments of this kind and the factionalism which has characterized and diminished the field in the past. Moreover, we have felt it important to devote equal amounts of space to 'theory' (Chapters 2 to 4) and 'practice' (Chapters 5 to 7) in order to set out a clear view of the field and the opportunities it offers. The result is the chapters that follow, which, we suggest, may be read in varying order depending on the priorities of the reader.

- *Chapter 2* discusses the treatment of the field in recent 'research methods' textbooks in education and in introductions to historical research, pointing to the limitations of these genres.
- *Chapter 3* traces the development of the field through the distinctive development internationally of history as an academic discipline and education as a field of study before exploring the prospects for a greater integration of the two traditions.
- *Chapter 4* examines the application of a range of different social science theories and techniques to the historical study of education, including their varying influence and plausibility.
- *Chapter 5* reviews the range of published and easily accessible sources that can be deployed by researchers in this field.
- *Chapter 6* investigates the use of less easily accessible types of evidence – unpublished documents, visual evidence and **oral sources** – as well as discussing quantitative analysis in historical study and ways of combining different types of sources and analysis in educational history.
- *Chapter 7* pulls together the conclusions drawn and questions raised by earlier chapters through discussion of the design and execution of historical research projects in education, including a set of problems and opportunities for study.

The text is designed to be read straight through, with each chapter building on the last in a discussion which becomes increasingly addressed to practical considerations. Equally, readers who wish to engage straight away with pragmatics can begin with Chapters 5 and 6, which discuss the raw materials of any historical project in education; then they can reflect on the positioning of their work and its interpretative assumptions through the questions raised in Chapters 2, 3 and 4, before applying these perspectives to the questions of research design and execution raised in Chapter 7.

Thinking historically

We have written this book partly in the conviction that historical research is an important means of understanding and addressing contemporary concerns. It can also illuminate the structures and the taken for granted assumptions of our contemporary world, by demonstrating that these have developed historically, that they were established for particular purposes that were often social, economic and political in nature, and that in many cases they are comparatively recent in their origin. This is important, for example, in shaping an understanding of what we mean by the currently fashionable phrase 'educational settings', which has been adopted for the series of which this book is a part. The establishment of state systems of schooling during the nineteenth and twentieth centuries encouraged a widespread assumption that the settings in which education takes place should normally be institutionalized, bureaucratic and age-specific. At the end of the twentieth century, the emergence of new ideas and policies designed to encourage 'lifelong learning' and a 'learning society' began to challenge this kind of assumption by suggesting that education can take place in a very wide range of settings, throughout life, for different social groups and within many kinds of formal and informal environments. Historical research can also highlight the pervasive and widespread nature of educational experience in different eras. By investigating the development of modern state-sanctioned educational systems, it can demonstrate that the nature of those systems was not inevitable and is not predetermined, or indeed immutable. It can shed light on the origins of contemporary practices and ideas that we have come to take for granted. And, not least, it can bring to our attention many agencies and arenas other than the modern school that also count and have counted as 'educational settings'.

Our current notions of school and education, then, are historical creations that came into being and became established for specific reasons that have much to do with their cultural surroundings. This same is true of particular types of school and forms of education, such as nursery schools, primary schools, secondary schools, apprenticeship, universities, technical and liberal education and adult education. The means that have been developed for providing education, such as lectures, seminars and classes, are also historically contingent, as are the methods for assessing their outcomes, such as examinations, tests and practical projects. The familiar **artefacts** of education, including desks, textbooks, blackboards, playgrounds and the very buildings constructed to accommodate them, are all historical inventions. No less so are ideas and practices that were once well established but were then abandoned, such as, in England, school galleries, the monitorial system and the eleven-plus examination. Understanding the origins of such phenomena, the ways in which they were regarded, the alternative forms and principles with which they were contrasted and the reasons for their resilience and ultimate decline is the basic purpose of historical research on education. In the process it is also possible to deconstruct what Tyack and Cuban (1995: 85) describe as the 'grammar of schooling', which has remained surprisingly consistent for decades and in some ways for centuries.

A good example of historical research in education, and more particularly the historically mediated nature of modern educational ideas and practices, concerns the idea of the school curriculum. Modern assumptions about the nature of the school curriculum and related ideas about classrooms can be traced in Europe in some detail to the early sixteenth century, while the creation of mass systems of schooling through textbooks, examinations and school subjects was a nineteenth-century refinement. Historical research has shed a great deal of light on how and why the curriculum assumed a recognizably modern form, as may be seen in Case study 1.

Case study 1: Historical research on the school curriculum and classroom

Ariès (1960) documents the origins of the school 'class' as dating back no further than the sixteenth or late fifteenth century, and not assuming a recognizably modern form until the beginning of the seventeenth. Documented for the first time in 1519 in a letter from Erasmus describing St Paul's School in London, it acquired many of its present day characteristics by the end of the sixteenth century in the Jesuits' *ratio studiorum* and the *leges et statuta* of the University of Paris, the curriculum being taught in specialist classes. Specific premises for each class (the classroom) were established in place of the single schoolroom, and Aries suggests that this reveals 'a realization of the special nature of childhood or youth and of the idea that within that childhood or youth a variety of categories existed' (p. 182).

Hamilton (1989) reports a slightly earlier usage of 'class' (1517) than that uncovered by Aries, and suggests that it emerged as a way to identify subdivisions within 'schools'. They helped to link schooling more clearly with bureaucratic and social control. He notes that the earliest use of the term 'curriculum' located by the *Oxford English Dictionary* is in the records of the University of Glasgow for 1633, but traces it back to sixteenth-century debates: 'First came the introduction of class divisions and closer pupil surveillance; and second came the refinement of pedagogic content and methods. The net result, however, was cumulative: teaching and learning became, for good or ill, more open to external scrutiny and control' (p. 49).

Reid (1990) portrays the emergence of the school 'curriculum' at the end of the sixteenth century in terms of the arrival of a more closely knit organization of educational activities, especially in the way that they were seen as sequential and capable of completion: 'Progression is the counterpart of completion and makes possible the idea of curriculum as an educational category' (p. 206). This reflects the work of Renaissance scholars such as Peter Ramus to make teaching and learning more systematic through applications of 'method'. The move away from loosely connected studies and towards curriculum is also related to a shift from studying texts to the use of textbooks, which had become available with the invention of printing.

Stray (1994) finds that whereas the term 'school book' dates from the late seventeenth century, 'textbook' does not appear until the 1830s. The school book of the eighteenth century was produced for use in instructional sequences; for example, a school edition of Shakespeare with notes to aid understanding. The textbook as it developed in the nineteenth century was a book designed to provide 'an authoritative pedagogic version of an area of knowledge' (p. 2), a 'specialised, manufactured commodity' (p. 8) for which there soon arose a distinct and organized market. In these conditions, there was strong competition between rival textbooks, but some became dominant. For example, Benjamin Kennedy's *The Public School Latin Primer* was first published in 1866 and held the field until 1888, when a radically revised primer appeared.

Kliebard (1996) presents a concrete example of the appearance of a concept of curriculum that went beyond that dictated by the textbook, and the rise of 'ensemble teaching' as distinct from teaching through monitoring individual recitations. He demonstrates these changes taking place from data relating to one country school in Columbia County, Wisconsin, in the United States in the second half of the nineteenth century. He links these developments to the introduction of age stratification as an organizational device across the United States, to suggest an 'intimate interrelationship' between management and organization on one hand, and pedagogical change on the other (p. 137).

Goodson (1988) sets out to show that the birth of secondary school examinations and the institutionalization of curriculum differentiation took place at almost the same time as each other in England in the mid-nineteenth century. According to Goodson, 'If "class and curriculum" entered educational discourse when schooling was transformed into a mass activity in England "classroom system and school subjects" emerged at the stage at which that mass activity became a state-subsidised system' (p. 29). A hierarchical pattern was established which, he maintains, forged a 'triple alliance' of academic subjects, academic examinations and able students. This in turn was used to justify a clear hierarchy in the allocation of status and resources.

In different periods of history and from their different analytical perspectives – childhood, pedagogy, institutions, economics, social relations – each of these researchers has sought to understand aspects of the evolution and development of the curriculum in schools. Separately and together, they help to inform an understanding of a set of educational ideas and practices, or 'settings'. Yet the episodic view of the curriculum in different eras generated by a range of such specialist studies is itself problematic. The research techniques deployed are varied and some studies are more securely grounded than others in the historical record. Moreover, as Nicholas Orme suggests, **continuity** in schooling is often neglected by historians more interested in establishing points of change. In several detailed studies, Orme has established the great longevity in England of many school processes often assumed to be of more modern origin: the school day was probably already formally structured in England in the twelfth century and detailed timetables survive from the 1440s; by the 1180s it is known that pupils of different schools competed against one another in public disputations where their learning was open to public examination; from around 1200 medieval schoolmasters began systematically to use class texts with their pupils, often abridging standard texts and providing commentaries as pedagogic aids; in the thirteenth century educationists began to specify in detail the skills training required of schoolboys of different ages; the professional schoolmaster in charge of his class and supervising bureaucratic processes such as enrolment is recorded by 1339; school books for the use of all pupils in class were printed in England from about 1483 and were an important part of the printing trade by 1500 (Orme 1973, 1984, 1989). In this light, Orme (1984: 238) contends, 'the history of education since 1500 has been, in one sense, simply the widening of this basis' developed in the medieval age.

The subject matter of history is everything that mankind has thought and done and Orme's studies serve as a reminder that educational history, though selective in theme, remains very wide in scope. Moreover, history is both a craft and an art, drawing on formal research conventions yet embracing all interpretative traditions. How is the researcher to find a way in this enormous landscape? How and where should boundaries be drawn around a research project? What analytical tools, working methods and raw materials are available and how are choices to be made among them? These are some of the questions which we shall be addressing in the remainder of this book.

2 | What the textbooks say – and what they don't

We begin our analysis of historical research in educational settings with three chapters which, in various ways, are designed to locate the field historically and intellectually, and to prompt in the researcher's mind some important questions. Within which academic tradition do I stand – wittingly or unwittingly – as a historian of education? Can I embrace more than one tradition in my work and satisfy their respective requirements? Which is my preferred approach to the historiography of education and what research design questions flow from this choice? In this chapter and in Chapter 3 we undertake an analysis of specific ways in which the field has been defined and debated by historians and educationists, while in Chapter 4 we illustrate how studies in the field have been conceived and carried out within various branches of the social sciences. These chapters combine narrative reconstruction and analysis of these themes. Our intention has been to provide readers with access to an extensive and wide-ranging historiographical and methodological literature, along with a set of tools with which they may assess our judgements and further explore areas of particular interest.

In setting about locating the field the present chapter discusses the treatment of 'history of education' in recent research textbooks in Britain and North America. In broad terms, we deal with two types of book: a large group of works that introduce a wide array of research methods in education, and a separate set of volumes designed to introduce themes and debates in historical research. In the following pages we discuss some of the useful and suggestive material for the historical study of education to be found in both types of text. Nevertheless, we consider this Anglo-American genre as a whole to be disappointing in its scope and ambition, notwithstanding its influence around the English-speaking world. First, the coverage of the field is uneven. Most often historical research in education is of marginal concern in both kinds of book. Rarely is it a substantive theme and a majority of such texts omit it entirely. Second, the existing literature of this kind is eclectic and idiosyncratic. As a result there is, we would contend, no entirely persuasive introductory survey which does justice to the complex relation of history and education.

Research methods in education

Since the earliest years of the twentieth century, American students have enrolled on masters and doctoral programmes in education and this readership has generated a steady flow of general textbooks introducing such students to the research methods employed in the field. With the spread of higher degrees internationally and the very rapid growth in enrolment after 1960 (Lagemann 1997: 6), this flow turned into a flood which has averaged one new title or revised edition every year since 1958 for the American market alone, accompanied by similar texts published elsewhere in the English-speaking world.

Such texts are often very practical, and tend to appeal to a mass market of teachers and education administrators. Most have assumed little or nothing in terms of prior research experience on the part of the reader. While some books of this genre treat educational research exclusively as an experimental science, many others allocate a chapter to historical research as one of a range of qualitative 'methods' or 'approaches' that can be adopted in educational research. In this section we review the latter kind of literature, concentrating in some detail on trends since the early 1970s. Summarized in brief, three main phases of such work may be noted.

- *The 1930s to early 1970s:* textbooks emphasize education as a progressive science within which appears a chapter on historical methods of research alongside chapters on other 'humanistic' or 'descriptive' methods.
- *The early 1970s to date:* most new textbooks relegate treatment of historical research to short sub-sections of material on descriptive or 'non-experimental' methods; new editions of existing textbooks retain separate chapters on historical research but few discuss recent developments in historiography and most are increasingly dated.
- *The mid-1980s to date:* some new textbooks, influenced by developments in broader 'social research' substitute for historical research descriptions of life-history, biographical, documentary, and oral history research; meanwhile a new genre of edited collections of essays on qualitative research methods, strongly influenced by the developing agenda of 'social research' has emerged.
  (*Source: content analysis of 51 editions of education research methods textbooks published in America and Britain since 1932.*)

For reasons that we will explore in Chapter 3, English language studies of education in the past were conducted overwhelmingly by educationists during the period 1900 to 1960, before this practice and the research methods and assumptions that supported it were subjected to trenchant criticism by academic historians. To this point successive generations of educational researchers were introduced to historical method by authors such as Carter V. Good (Good *et al.* 1936; Good and Scates 1954; Good 1959, 2nd edn 1963), who diligently discussed mainstream historical method – especially the identification of sources and their critique – while, in progressive vein, emphasizing the 'functional character' of historical research in education, 'where the purpose is to profit by the experiences of the past in the solution of present-day problems' (Good *et al.* 1936: 239–40). From the late 1950s a growing list of rival American volumes took a similar line, typified by Van Dalen (1962), who broke down the procedures of historical research into five separate processes: 'selecting the problem', 'collecting source materials', 'criticizing source materials', 'formulating hypotheses to explain events and conditions' and 'interpreting and reporting findings'.

In itself, the model was sound enough as an anatomy of traditional historical method. The problem lay in the guidance provided about its application and the results obtained. Most textbook authors set out a sequential and unproblematic set of procedures to be followed in a manner not dissimilar to the 'scientific' methods discussed in other chapters, culminating in a research 'report'. The possibility of widely divergent aims and interpretative assumptions and how these might affect research design were ignored and the result, as a highly critical group of academic historians began pointing out in the 1960s, was an unsophisticated, chronicling and present-oriented tradition of historical research in university departments of education. In the face of this assault, for the first time in the twentieth century educationists specializing in history found themselves ceding ground to the professional interest of academic historians. The effect of this external challenge can be gauged through the treatment accorded to historical study in education research methods texts. Some authors have opted for retrenchment, while others have attempted to alter significantly discussion of the purpose and scope of historical material in educational research.

The retrenchment has taken two forms. First, a growing half-heartedness has crept into many treatments of this theme. We need not dwell on texts where historical research has been relegated to as little as one page out of three hundred (Slavin 1984: 71–2). Little comment is required other than the complete inadequacy of the treatment. Nevertheless, this kind of debasement is a general trend of the past 30 years, usually taking one of two forms: downgraded to one element in a general treatment of 'non-experimental' or 'descriptive' research methods (see, for example, Skager and Weinberg 1971; Slavin 1984; Charles 1988; Wiseman 1999); or, alternatively, discussed briefly as one of three approaches to researching education alongside descriptive and experimental method (Turney and Robb 1971; Verma and Beard 1981; Eichelberger 1989; Verma and Mallick 1999). Such texts – typically three to eight pages in length – may satisfy their authors' desire for comprehensive coverage but in their cursory discussion they signal a retreat, leaving the field free to academic historians and discouraging students of educational studies from undertaking historical research at all. Some authors, such as Asher (1976), have explicitly dissuaded such students from entering the field: 'those committed to the scholarly study of educational processes and problems are best advised to avoid historical research problems unless they have been thoroughly trained as historians' (p. 152). Others have taken the view that historical research method no longer warrants discussion at all. Thus, an extensive British guide to educational research, edited by Peter Gordon, an experienced historian of education, excludes entirely such treatment in favour of themes based mainly on the subjects of the new National Curriculum (Gordon 1996).

A second form of retrenchment is that of newer textbooks or updated editions of older works that still give a full chapter to historical research but show limited awareness of contemporary developments in historiography. A majority of such treatments found currently on the shelves of university libraries are scarcely adequate for current conditions. Most have ignored or touch only briefly on the challenge to educationists posed by academic historians in the 1960s, which we discuss in Chapter 3. As a result, such textbook treatments have become increasingly vulnerable to fundamental criticism. Furthermore, when a second wave of controversy in general historiography – also discussed in the next chapter – began to gather momentum in the 1980s and have an impact on the writing of educational history, this too was ignored. Consequently, versions of the treatment first developed in the 1930s still appear in new texts and revised books, their practical value for historians of education being limited and their contribution to broader historiographical literature being negligible (for example: in the UK, Cohen and Manion 1980, 4th edn 1994; in North America, Wiersma 1969, 4th edn 1986; Fraenkel and Wallen 1990, 3rd edn 1996; Anderson 1990, 2nd edn 1998). The most significant failure of such texts has been the absence of a problematic approach to the interpretation of historical sources in the light of contemporary historiographical debate. Only a handful – those incorporated into our discussion in Chapter 3 and included in the recommended reading at the end of Chapter 7 – have risen above the assertion of a rigid, sequential and essentially static model of historical research divorced from the central controversies and practical choices that have faced working historians over the past three decades.

Meanwhile, in a development separate from the two forms of retrenchment just described, the past 15 years have witnessed the emergence of a third trend in the content of education research methods texts. These are surveys of a new form of historical study which is strongly reliant on a combination of the fieldwork methods of qualitative research in the social sciences, now generally termed 'social research', and critical theory. This new form, only loosely inspired by traditional historical method, is variously labelled 'life history', 'biography', 'policy' and **'narrative' research**. It takes some of the traditional interests and skills of the historian – chronological analysis, the biographical subject, the policy process and narrative writing – and applies them to **social theory** in education. While all authorities are agreed that these methods are descriptive and predominantly qualitative (opposed to scientific or experimental), there is debate about the extent to which they are rooted in the traditional 'humanistic' method of history or in the techniques and interpretative frames of social science. In practice a large majority of contemporary educationists are more interested in, comfortable with and competent to undertake the latter methodology; moreover, most are also content to combine at will research methods and techniques from very different traditions. In the main, discussion of these working methods remains almost absent in general research methods textbooks. Instead it is represented in a mushrooming form of parallel literature, the edited collection of essays concerned with qualitative research in education.

An early British example of the new genre was the work edited by Burgess (1985), which devoted four of its eleven chapters on qualitative methods in educational research to different aspects of historical method. Burgess was hopeful that these historical contributions could help to show how the 'data and methods' associated with historical research might complement other approaches to understanding education, and even 'overcome some of the deficiencies in observational and interview material' (p. 14). Goodson (1985) opened the discussion by considering the use of life stories and how to integrate studies of historical **context**, with the purpose of 'exploring the role of historical studies in redressing certain emergent tendencies within qualitative methods' (p. 121). The pursuit of historical data, he suggested, could 'open up the prospect of developing cognitive maps of process and of decision-making, of individuals and interest groups at work over time', and would also allow access to 'the recurrent patterns and powerful legacies on which all contemporary action must build' (p. 125). Placing himself in a long-standing educationist tradition, Goodson emphasized that the prime purpose of studying the history was to address current educational problems. In the same volume, Andrew (1985) pursued this aim further through an investigation of problems involved in the collection, analysis and use of historical documentary evidence. Purvis (1985) followed this with reflections on undertaking historical documentary research from a feminist perspective. Lastly, Saran (1985) focused on the use of archives and interviews in research on educational policy.

Andrew and Purvis were especially frank about their lack of experience in historical research. For example, Andrew reflected on her own confusions over historical method as well as difficulties in getting to grips with the relevant historical literature on a topic, and developed a useful discussion of the issues involved when a researcher from the social sciences uses historical sources for the first time:

The collection, analysis and use of historical documentary evidence raises methodological issues and problems for all researchers, while the sociologist involved in historical research faces further difficulties and dilemmas brought about by the often uncomfortable straddling of two separate academic disciplines . . . The would-be historical sociologist with an initial training in sociology faces the task of self-education as a historian before the research project can proceed.

(Andrew 1985: 153–4)

Purvis (1985: 186) also comments that she well remembers her 'bewilderment, and yet excitement' when she first began reading documents of different kinds about her chosen historical study, not having undertaken any historical research before.

Perhaps the single most useful sources where these new quasi-historical research methods in education are laid alongside others more indicative of twentieth-century research as a whole are the two editions of *Educational Research, Methodology and Development: an International Handbook*, edited by John Keeves in 1988 and 1997. Keeves comments that the fast changing configuration of educational research necessitated considerable changes to the second edition of the work in which 156 separate essays are brought together from across the English-speaking world. These include seven contributions relevant to the present discussion:

1 *Humanistic research methods*
  - biographical research methods (by N. K. Denzin);
  - educational history in biographies and autobiographies (by T. Husen);
  - historical methods in educational research (by C. F. Kaestle);
  - narrative enquiry (by F. M. Connelly and D. J. Clandinin);
  - oral history (by B. K. Hyams).
2 *Critical theory, policy research and evaluation*
  - policy analysis (by M. Trow);
  - policy-oriented research (by J. Nisbet).

As editor, Keeves held the view that the first five methods were best grouped as 'humanistic', being designed to 'provide understanding and an interpretative account of educational phenomena', while the two remaining were indicative of a separate form of educational research which is concerned with 'the introduction of change through social action', including policy (Keeves 1997: xvi–xvii). Keeves also insisted that 'educational research possesses a unity that extends across different disciplinary perspectives' through its search for any form of knowledge 'that is available for transforming the real world through human agency and social action' (p. xv). Here, then, is a fundamentally progressive understanding of the nature and purpose of educational research, in which disciplinary boundaries matter less than the ends to which research is directed (although its defining characteristics are dependent on core constructs from sociology). It is also a formulation emblematic of a new confidence that educational research can escape at last from its uncertain status within universities by showing itself to be self-evidently useful. This is a far remove from the cautious stance of even recent research methods textbooks, in which educational research is depicted in a passive relationship to other forms of knowledge: 'educational researchers have relied heavily on research techniques used in other disciplines. It is only the educational nature of the research question that distinguishes educational research from that in other fields' (Crowl 1996: 198).

Yet the claims made by those championing new qualitative research methods of education can easily move from confidence to recklessness. Throughout the twentieth century education was a poor relation to history in the university (see Chapter 3) and there is much in the new literature on qualitative methods that is historically crude and unsophisticated as well as cavalier, courting a damaging backlash from academic historians. Ironically, there is a historical lesson here. By the late 1970s academic historians had for two decades been highly critical of much historical work undertaken by educationists (see Chapter 3). This was one influence on the decision of the American Educational Research Association (AERA) to declare its dissatisfaction with existing American-based educational research textbooks and contribute a work of its own, edited by Jaeger (1988). The resulting volume concentrated heavily in its opening section on historical research in education, and pointed out that whereas existing educational research textbooks tended to have an 'overemphasis on quantitative methods', historical inquiry and method were generally addressed with 'comparative superficiality' (p. i). The substantive chapter on 'Historical methods in educational research' contributed by Carl Kaestle (see Chapter 7) was a sophisticated analysis of educational historiography from a traditional standpoint. Another, earlier, by-product of the AERA's initiative was a collection, edited by Best (1983), which laid out an agenda for historical research in American education.

The AERA agenda was already being overtaken, however. By now the rise of the 'social research' perspective was rapidly gaining ground in literature on education research method. This has generated a new kind of textbook, such as that by Hitchcock and Hughes (1989, 2nd edn 1995), the coverage of which includes life history and documentary research. The emphasis here is on the biographical or oral history interview as one of a number of interview techniques in 'social and educational research' (1995: 184). According to the authors, the main value of this research method is to elucidate 'the significant influence of personal biography on teaching and learning' and to raise questions concerning 'the intersection of an individual life with the social structure, or cultural and organisational processes' (pp. 209–10). If these priorities seem at some remove from the traditional method of the academic historian, Hitchcock and Hughes reinforce the point by emphasizing the place of oral and life history firmly in the domain of cultural studies and critical theory rather than history: ' "writing" is firmly on the agenda in qualitative research traditions . . . More and more educational research journals are accepting different styles of presenting research and its findings. There has been a large increase in the number of confessional tales in educational research' (p. 339). In the 1990s this was a trend with which the AERA had to wrestle. One result is the collection on educational biography edited by Kridel (1998), in which seven of the contributions were first presented to members of the AERA's special interest group in archival and biographical research. A decade on from Kaestle's consideration of traditional documentary method in historical research, Kridel pointed to the detachment of recent educational research from any secure grounding in traditional historical method: 'much current writing in the field of education . . . draws upon important work in the social sciences and attends primarily to matters of narrative, life-history, story telling, voice and autobiography. Psychology, feminist studies, critical theory, anthropology and sociology are all well represented with only marginal references to the humanities' (p. 4).

That this kind of research now predominates in literature on research methods in education is indicated in the selection by Keeves (1997) – already mentioned – in which, of seven historically orientated themes, only Kaestle's reprinted essay and Husen's contribution address the traditional methods of documentary history. The most recent edited collections and textbooks serve to reinforce the point. For example, Scott and Usher's collection of 1996 includes a sociological chapter on biographical method (Erben 1996; see also Erben 1998) and the same editors' textbook (1999) emphasizes the place of philosophical issues in educational research, includes a chapter of 'biographical and autobiographical method', but has no discussion of historical research. Meanwhile, other recent collections on qualitative research methods in education contain 'reflexive' accounts of their authors' experiences influenced by contemporary fashions in critical theory. They are similarly silent on historical method when such a contextual perspective might have served to offset the air of narcissism which can pervade such texts (see, for example, Walford 1991, 1998; Halpin and Troyna 1994).

Finally, some texts not only marginalize historical study but explicitly question its epistemological value. For example, on no less a platform than his presidential address to the British Educational Research Association in 1991, Bassey argued that historical research has little to offer education. 'In the past there has been too much slavish repetition in education, following the historical method; today there is too much blind playing of hunches' (Bassey 1992: 3). Warming further to his theme in 1995, Bassey went on to distinguish what he called 'educational research' from sociological, psychological, historical and philosophical research in education. 'It is particularly important', he declared, 'that educational research be recognised as research that aims critically to inform educational judgements and decisions in order to improve educational action, while sociological, psychological, historical and philosophical research in education are concerned critically to inform understandings of discipline-pertinent phenomena in educational settings' (1995: 39). Research in educational settings, Bassey argued, is only 'educational research' if it is 'concerned with attempts to improve educational judgements and decisions' (p. 37). Here, then, we come full circle. Bassey bids educationists retreat to the progressive, **ahistorical**, scientific model for educational research of the early decades of the twentieth century. It is the very model which early proponents of historical research methods in education such as Carter Good challenged as inadequate in the 1930s.

Overall, the kind of educational research methods literature that we have surveyed fails to provide a balanced and considered introduction for students wishing to undertake historical research in education. The traditional textbook approach which Good promoted has become increasingly threadbare over the past two decades, while the emergence of a new literature on qualitative research methods in education has relegated the traditional historical skills of documentary analysis to the margin. Yet this tradition remains the bedrock of academic history, an enterprise which, over the same period, has taken an unprecedented interest in the history of education. Accordingly, it is to this field and its introductory literature that we now turn.

Introductions to historical research

The research methods texts that have been so characteristic of the field of educational research are much less common and do not typify those in historical research. In the first place, academic history is a much smaller field. In England as recently as 1991 two-fifths of all university teachers of history were employed in one of three universities: Oxford, Cambridge and London (Stevenson 1993: 71–2). Moreover, until the past decade or so academic history was a relatively autonomous, homogeneous discipline little disturbed by methodological dispute. The small number of full-time graduate students who had won highly competitive scholarships and the even smaller number who went on to teach in the universities saw little need to publish essays on their working methods.

Second, while some professional historians have written about their craft, these books have, in the main, been philosophical (Carr 1961), polemical (Elton 1967) or reflective essays (Hexter 1961; Evans 1997), rather than manuals. Most recently, for reasons more fully explored in Chapter 3, the influence of 'postmodernism' has produced an expanding new genre of general, often radical, texts focusing on the standing of historical knowledge and its uses (for example, Young 1990; Jenkins 1995) and the more recent introductions to the study of history now tend to refer to 'a growing literature on the theoretical problems raised by historical study and research' (Butler 1997: 31). Even so, as Tosh notes (2000 [1984]: 215–16),

> Historians are not much given to reflecting on the nature of their discipline . . . Firstly there are the personal statements by distinguished historians which are often very illuminating but make no claim to be comprehensive . . . The second approach is to raise questions to do with the nature and scope of history through the history of historical writing, or assessments of individual historians . . . Apart from these two categories, there are very few satisfactory introductory works.

In the introductions to historical research and historiography that have been produced, issues relating to education have usually been conspicuous by their absence. This is true, for example, of Barzun and Graff (1957, 5th edn 1992), for four decades a leading introductory text in America.

In the British context there are some short introductions available that are directed at sixth-formers and history undergraduates. These explain some of the key terms and traditions of history, and how to approach writing essays, examinations and short dissertations (see, for example, Brown and Daniels 1986; Abbott 1996; Black and Macraild 1997). Tosh (2000 [1984]) is, perhaps, the single most useful general introduction. This work is aimed at history undergraduates undertaking 'introductory courses on the methods and scope of history' (p. viii), but includes much of value for more experienced historians, including discussions on assessing and understanding **primary sources,** and the implications for all working historians of contemporary themes in historiography, writing and composition. Also valuable is the collection edited by Butler and Gorst (1997), which aims to identify for postgraduate students 'the areas of principal interest to those beginning historical research, especially areas involving the identification, location and organisation of primary materials, and the problems involved in presenting research findings' (p. x). To achieve this the collection includes essays on historical writing, the relation of theory and practice, computing techniques, research management and funding and 'the Internet for historians'.

Academic historians, then, are reawakening as a profession to the challenge of undertaking systematic scrutiny of their working methods, much in the manner of a similar scrutiny undertaken at the turn of the twentieth century. Then, as now, education as a theme barely featured in their deliberations. Nevertheless, there is some recent material available and in the remainder of this section we review a wide range of contemporary, mainly British, historiographical work broken down into the following genres: general historiographical surveys; education as a theme in oral and local history; case studies of educational historiography; and encyclopaedias, companions and dictionaries.

General historiographical surveys

Since the early 1980s, professional historians have generated a substantial historiographical literature but in a large majority of such works there is little or no reference to education as a field of enquiry. It is rare in a general historiographical text produced in Britain to find questions such as those posed by Burke (1991: 10) in a discussion of social history:

> If 'popular culture', for instance, is the culture of 'the people', who are the people? . . . Are they the illiterate or the uneducated? We cannot assume that economic, political or cultural divisions in a given society necessarily co-incide. And what is education? Is it only the training handed out in certain official institutions like schools and universities? Are ordinary people uneducated or do they simply have a different education, a different culture from elites?

More commonly education is all but omitted from the frame of reference. For example, in the most comprehensive modern historiographical surveys to have been produced in America and Britain the coverage is very thin. In the imposing volume edited for the American Historical Association by Kammen (1980) there is a short reference to the 'scattered American efforts' of the 1970s in the 'topical subfield' of education, especially those studies that attempted to apply a model of social control to nineteenth-century schooling (Stearns 1980: 215–16, 222–3). Brief attention is also given to women's education in the broader context of historical work on women and the family (Degler 1980: 321–2). Meanwhile, in a more recent and even larger British volume (Bentley 1997), discussion of historical writing on education is virtually absent, with merely a brief reference to work on twentieth century Japanese education reform (see Smith 1997: 669).

Similarly, when one turns to those introductory texts which analyse a range of contemporary sub-fields within history, education barely features, even in those themes where it might seem of central concern. Table 2.1 gives two such British examples with notes on the very minor reference made to educational themes.

Despite the prevailing absence of educational history as a theme in general historiographical surveys, there are some specific contexts within which it arises in such literature. In particular, a number of texts refer to the development of history as a disciplinary field, over a very wide period and in an international context. These include: Gransden (1982) on historical writing in medieval England; Hay (1977: 94–7) on the role of the historian in fifteenth-century Italy; Fussner (1962: 45–8) on history in the secondary schools and universities of sixteenth- and seventeenth-century England; Kenyon (1983) on historians and the historical profession in England since the sixteenth century; Bentley (1997: 406–7) on history in German universities of the eighteenth century; Forbes (1952: 114–17) on history in the

Figure 2.1 The sub-fields of history: two recent British surveys

Burke (1991)	Gardiner (1988)
The 'New History'	Military history
History from below	Political history
Women's history	Economic history
Overseas history	Social history[b]
Microhistory	Religious history
Oral history[a]	History of science[c]
History of reading	Women's history[d]
History of images	Intellectual history
History of political thought	History of popular culture
History of the body	Diplomatic history
History of events and the revival	European history
of narrative	Third world history

[a] Mentions work on children's lore and discusses history teaching in contemporary schools.
[b] Mentions education as a theme.
[c] Mentions academies of science.
[d] Mentions literacy, the family and apprenticeship.

secondary schools and universities of nineteenth-century England; Parker (1990) on history in British universities since the nineteenth century; Hertzberg (1980: 474–504) on the history of history teaching in nineteenth- and twentieth-century American secondary schools, colleges and universities; and Birmingham (1997: 703–4) on African history in British universities in the 1960s. Thus the shared interest of such works in educational issues is largely restricted to a desire to plot the origins and development of the historical profession itself.

Oral and local history

One branch of historiographical literature in which there is fairly wide discussion of education is oral history. In broad terms, this takes two forms. First, oral history is often examined for its use as an educational tool in schools and universities. For example, Perks (1990) provides 32 published case studies of **oral history** used in the school curriculum (not only in history), and 45 resource packs produced for use in British schools. Complementing this, Thompson (1988: 8–11, 166–84) gives an extended assessment of the educational value of undertaking oral history in schools, colleges and adult education classes. In so doing he stresses the potential of oral history projects to support child-centred learning (p. 9) and skills development involving the collection of evidence, inquiry, language, technical and social skills (pp. 167–9). The most spectacular success story of this sort is the Foxfire project, started in a school in Georgia, USA. During 1972–8, this school's oral history publications sold over four million copies and spawned more than 200 similar high school magazines across America.

A second form of discussion about the role of education in oral history concerns those projects in which participants' memories of schools, teachers and childhood are prominent. Perks (1990), for example, has details of 57 oral history projects on the experience of schooling in the United Kingdom that were undertaken during 1945–89, mainly since the early 1970s, together with several on school strikes and teachers. In addition, a large number of projects are reported on childhood in general, including children's games, gangs, homes, rhymes and songs inspired by the pioneering of modern research of this kind by Iona and Peter Opie (1959; see also Caunce 1994; Howarth 1998).

In addition to oral history there is some mention in recent British reference works to the place of education in the burgeoning field of local history. Hey (1998), for example, discusses various approaches to the historical study of apprenticeship, children and education, including detailed discussion of the location and availability of a wide range of primary source material (see also Stephens 1981; Friar 1991; Herber 1997). However, as this field has grown over recent decades tensions have developed around it, with many professional historians disdaining local history as 'amateur'. Attempting to escape this problem, the journal *Amateur Historian* (launched in 1952 and featuring a steady flow of articles on education) changed its name in 1968 to *Local Historian*. As with education in oral history, there are two main forms of education in local history. Its emergence as an educational tool in schools and teacher training colleges is discussed, for example, in Douch (1965), Skipp (1967), Phelps *et al.* (1974–5), and Davies (1974–5). Moreover, many studies of education from a local history perspective have been undertaken in Britain by professional historians, educationists, history undergraduates and adult 'enthusiasts'. This last category of work has grown dramatically in size since the 1980s through the extension of adult education, the availability of more freely accessible archives and increasing early retirement, which provides more opportunity for cultural pursuits (Moss 1997). Local history in both forms is still treated with disdain in some quarters. For example, Moss (1997: 964) suggests:

school children have become in the 1990s research students without the necessary methodological skills or framework of historical reference. The undergraduate syllabus has been similarly transformed with greater emphasis on dissertations and the exploration of historical data. As a result archivists have found themselves having to provide advice and guidance to pupils and students in search of the novel rather than the attainable . . . and even national record offices [have become] driven by the needs of enthusiasts, who in the post-war liberal world expected access to be free to all documents, whether public or private.

Case studies of educational historiography

Case studies in the historiography of education are very few and far between. Two British examples are Drake (1973) and Youngman (1978). As the editor of a collection of 'applied historical studies' for The Open University, Drake chose as one case study three articles from *Economic History Review* in which E. G. West and J. S. Hurt debated combatively resource allocation and statistics in early nineteenth-century British education and the value to the historian of surviving **documentary sources** on this theme. As soon as West's interpretation of published statistics appeared in print it was challenged by Hurt, who wrote a critique designed to show that the material on which West had based his arguments was 'of little value to the historian' (Drake 1973: 105). As editor of the reader Drake used this exchange and West's reply to make a set of general historiographical points. First, he suggested that if West's published primary sources were of doubtful value there were other sources in 'the various educational returns' held at the Public Record Office against which they could be tested, in particular questionnaires completed by all elementary schools seeking government support from 1846 onwards. Moreover, for the period 1857–1946 the files – some 68,000 of them – were seemingly 'complete, none having been weeded or thrown away' (Drake 1973: 5). Drake makes the claim that such 'large deposits of data suitable for analysis by social scientists' can be 'superior to what the contemporary world can supply' (pp. 7–8), and for him this example from the official education archive is an ideal illustration of the potential of applied historical study, which he defines as 'explorations of the past undertaken with the explicit purpose of advancing social scientific enquiries . . . [This is] a task which involves a search for appropriate historical data; the devising of ways to exploit it and, not least important, the presentation of findings in a form acceptable to social scientists' (p. 1).

A second case study example (Youngman 1978) comprises a useful analysis of four historical projects on education, comprising sixteenth- to nineteenth-century examples of research into pedagogy, biography, educational institutions and local history. It is written for prospective masters and doctoral students, and shows how five authors set about identifying a subject of historical research in education, finding and analysing primary sources, broadening the range of sources as a project develops, interpreting sources in context and drawing conclusions from the whole project. Emphasis is also placed on practical matters, such as planning the timetable of a project. It acknowledges that the work can be laborious: 'one must accept that a great deal of historical research can be most tedious' (p. 18). It also discusses accessing widely dispersed primary sources, recording and organizing primary source material, choosing start and end points in the **chronology** of the study, clarity of writing and the isolating nature of such research. It points out soberly that 'it is unfashionable now to point to one all important characteristic of good scholarship, namely that of hard graft ... Not least, the writing of a thesis in the history of education, particularly if pursued on a part-time basis, demands the encouragement and understanding of one's family and friends' (p. 29).

Encyclopaedias, companions and dictionaries

The final kind of historiographical literature that it is useful to review is historical encyclopaedias, companions and dictionaries, many of the most imposing and ambitious examples of which are prepared in the United States. In the main these works set out merely to summarize for the general reader factual information on a range of themes, including education (for example, Strayer 1982–9; Saul 1983; Cannon 1997; Mitchell 1998; Szarmach *et al.* 1998). However, in a small number of cases they include entries which contain useful historiographical analysis.

A prominent example edited in Britain is the *Blackwell Dictionary of Historians* (Cannon *et al.* 1988), which, as the title suggests, 'contains over 450 biographical entries which indicate the scholarly reputation of historians, the circumstances in which they worked and the extent to which their work has subsequently been confirmed or refuted' (Preface). In addition, there are articles on the historiography characteristic of different regions of the world, and entries covering technical terms used by working historians and genres of history. As in the general historiographical surveys discussed above, there is little direct reference to education in the *Dictionary*. The history of education fails to have its own entry yet there are some useful pointers scattered throughout the volume. The American historian Bernard Bailyn is credited with having made a 'profound impact' on educational historiography, which 'led historians of education to redefine their subject' (p. 29) (see also our discussion in Chapter 3); English local history (discussed above) is singled out as having made a particular contribution to the history of education (p. 252); the influence on historians of sociologists in emphasizing 'the importance of what they call the "reproduction" of society in the family, in schools, at work and elsewhere' is highlighted (p. 387) (see Chapter 4); the breadth of the interests of R. H. Tawney, including his having written extensively on education throughout his life, is noted (see Chapter 5); and the influence of the 'prolific and controversial' Lawrence Stone is analysed, drawing attention to his work on literacy and education (p. 392) (see Chapters 3 and 6), as is the work of Phillipe Ariès on the history of childhood (see Chapter 4) and Peter Laslett on the history of the family and the household (see Chapter 6).

Of all the recent works falling within this category, among the most significant for historians of education – and educational settings broadly defined – is the *Encyclopedia of Social History* (Stearns 1994), which includes the subject areas 'children' (eight entries, including 'youth'), 'education' (nine entries), 'family' (32 entries), 'gender' (23 entries), 'leisure' (16 entries) and 'methodology' (52 entries). In each case, entries are concerned as much with historiographical debates and controversies as with presenting straight historical information, and the influence of constructs and theories from social science is much in evidence. The starting point of the editor is that social history 'has become one of the key sources of expanding knowledge about human social behaviour', including its influence on sociology (p. vii). In the entry on education – largely devoted to schools in the West since 1800 – this overall approach is exemplified by Peter V. Meyers:

> scholars have increasingly delved into the complicated relationships between schools and society, examining education's contributions to social transformation, its response to societal change, and the social forces at work in the development of educational systems . . . Prior to the rise of social history most historians of education, assuming that the extension of schooling to the masses was beneficial and progressive, studied this development in terms of pedagogic theory and the political actions that were responsible for it. When social historians began to examine this period, they adopted a fundamentally different focus, trying to determine which groups, and what motives, were behind the creation of these new schools.
>
> (Stearns 1994: 210)

As may be inferred, the tone – and the role accorded to social history in general – is somewhat heroic in the *Encyclopedia*. As with the essays in all such volumes, what is omitted is as significant as what is included. Nevertheless, this work is very wide-ranging and indicative of a genre which, over the past two decades, has exerted a major influence over historical writing about education.

Conclusions

Both in the educational research methods literature and in works of historiography, the treatment of historical research in education has often been shallow and cursory or problematic. Within the genre of educational research methods textbooks, historical study has usually been discussed in a perfunctory and superficial fashion, and recently this coverage has been marginalized further. Meanwhile, contemporary introductions to academic history and historiography most commonly ignore education, except in relation to the evolution of the historical profession itself. In both spheres over the past two decades there have been isolated pockets of interest, especially in the educational literature on qualitative research – although the methodological analysis is often weak and credulous – while, in the burgeoning historiographical literature, education has made some impact in specific specialisms, such as oral history, local history and social history. Overall, however, historical research in education is portrayed misleadingly as dormant rather than active and it has little profile in either sphere. Such a situation requires explanation. In the next chapter, we seek to provide this through an account of the historical development of 'history' and 'education' as separate academic traditions. Only in this light, we contend, is it possible to understand why the specialist field of 'history of education' has been conceived so tentatively in the past and how it might be developed in the future.

3 | History or education?

In this chapter we raise a set of general questions about the nature of historical enquiry and its application within the field of education before, in later chapters, we discuss the contribution of concepts and techniques in social science to the history of education (Chapter 4) and the nature of the sources for historical research in education (Chapters 5 and 6). The inclusion of the present chapter is an acknowledgement of the recent burgeoning of historiographical literature about the nature and practice of historical writing. It is also intended as a response to the inadequacy, in our view, of most existing treatments of the historiography of education in the introductory texts surveyed in Chapter 2. Our aim in this and the chapters that follow is to help to clarify the scope and purpose of historical research in education as well as to throw light both on how it has been practised to the present and how it might be developed with more assurance in the future.

This is not to suggest that practising historians of education have been silent about their intentions or shy in advancing various definitions of the field. For example, influential statements about the purpose and scope of historical studies in education have been made in the USA and the UK over the past 40 years by prominent figures such as Bernard Bailyn, Lawrence Cremin, Lawrence Stone, Asa Briggs, Brian Simon and Harold Silver, and these are discussed below in this chapter. Moreover, it is also true that since the 1930s at least, in both countries there has been an uneasy tension between those – usually academic historians – who have espoused a liberal arts view of the value of educational history for its own sake and others – educationists, in the main – who have wanted to see historical studies in education put to use in addressing contemporary problems and controversies (Silver 1983: x). In practice this tension has often been implicit but in this book we have made it an explicit theme. Furthermore, where the USA and the UK has led historiographically, other Anglophone countries – Canada, Australia and New Zealand – have tended to follow, notwithstanding that the context of each country has resulted in the emergence of historiographical agendas that are revealingly distinctive (Spaull 1981: 2–5; Wilson 1984: 1–3; Openshaw *et al.* 1993: 12–15). These, too, are part of the analysis of this chapter.

The extent to which it is inevitable that there should be opposing liberal arts versus applied approaches to the writing of educational history is a useful starting point for our discussion. Is the study of education intrinsically concerned with advancing notions of social progress? To what extent is academic history an innately conservative discipline? In a field such as educational history how diverse is the audience and what are its varied expectations? To begin to answer these questions it is important to consider the nature of history as an academic discipline and education as a field of study. We discuss this in the first part of the chapter before moving to an examination of the problems and opportunities encountered by those studying the history of education, including issues of definition. In the concluding section we explore the extent to which a synthesis between the historical and educational research traditions is possible and of value.

The discipline of history

In recent years a large historiographical literature has emerged in the English speaking countries, especially the United States. Inevitably, this has had an impact on teaching as well as research, and if there has been one general trend in British undergraduate history it has been the emergence of compulsory courses in historiography. Much of the literature supporting such courses (for example, Butler 1997) implies that a critical perspective on the writing of history is a recent phenomenon, but this is manifestly false. In the late eighteenth century intellectuals east of the Rhine, under the influence of Immanuel Kant, were asserting that the past can never be reconstructed. All we can do, they maintained, is to construct in our present an image of the past testable through the internal consistency of the various sources that have survived to us. During the ensuing two centuries no other strain of thinking has proved so influential in shaping attitudes to historiography and, indeed, the test of internal consistency of sources has remained the touchstone of the historical enterprise (Bentley 1997: 406–9). Given such continuity, why has there been a movement in recent years to reassert strongly the subjectivity of historians in their dealings with historical evidence? To answer this question requires an examination of the rise of a historical profession, and through this means it is possible to discern the relation of insitutionalized history and socio-political change (see Slee 1988: 343–4).

'German' scholarship in the period 1780–1820 developed in the context of considerable upheaval. Political, social and economic revolutions were transforming Europe. In their wake intellectuals became increasingly interested in the processes of change and development in human character and institutions. In such a climate the concept of context began to replace that of fixed laws in discussions about the reasonable conduct of human affairs. And to study context some scholars began to use documentary evidence much more systematically than hitherto, borrowing, in the process, techniques from the adjacent disciplines of law, philology and biblical study. In this way the technical foundation for an emergent academic specialism began to be put in place. History was separate from philosophy in its distinctive use of sources, from archaeology in its concern with post-literate society and from antiquarianism in that it emphasized interpretation of national history rather than a collection of facts about local history. Moreover, an emphasis on national history was of further importance in the nineteenth century, in that it reflected the development of the nation state, with its associated national archives and official records which historians helped to calendar and proceeded to exploit. Increasingly historians were based in universities, first in states undergoing reconstruction (Berlin made its first appointment in history in 1810, Paris in 1812) and later in more stable countries (undergraduate history was first formally taught in England in 1848 and the USA in the 1870s). By 1900 historians were well established in leading universities internationally, their role, in part, being to transmit to both a professional and lay audience 'objective' national narratives based on the 'scientific' deployment of documentary sources (Slee 1988).

During the twentieth century this role persisted, with some modification, until quite recently. To take the UK as an example, the history profession remained small and tight-knit into the 1950s, numbering perhaps 400 university academics (Cannadine 1987: 171). The main subject continued to be political and institutional history (especially government and the church) and much of the emphasis was on continuity rather than change in the institutions of society. The medieval period in which such institutions flourished carried much weight, institutional longevity being seen as a sign of maturity, even superiority, among nation states, and this was one of the motivations behind important early studies in the history of education. A. F. Leach (a non-university 'amateur') undertook extensive original research designed to establish the medieval origins of the English grammar school (Leach 1896, 1911); Hastings Rashdall's two-volume history of European medieval universities (1895, revised in three volumes 1935) remains the standard work on this subject.

Only slowly was there diversification into other fields and only vaguely was there a developing self-consciousness among historians of the broader intellectual milieu of their enterprise. In the UK economic history was the first field beyond 'high' politics to establish itself with a specialist journal (1927). Others followed in the two decades after the war: ecclesiastical history (1950), social history (1952), medical history (1957), business history

(1958), labour history (1960) and the history of science (1962). Moreover, the tone of most historical writing was conservative, in that it was geographically insular, avoided methodological controversy, was designed to elaborate a common national identity and concentrated on a very small segment of society – the governing and intellectual classes. Historians were well entrenched in leading institutions: Oxford, Cambridge and London. Links to high-status schools – grammar and independent – were very strong. The profession encountered no methodological criticism from other university disciplines. Thus, as late as the early 1960s, the outward appearance of the historical profession in the UK was of a cohesive professional body largely united in its sense of purpose (Richardson 1999a).

To a considerable extent this was also true on the inside. Although they eschewed the label, nearly all historians from the 1930s to the 1960s in Western universities were 'modernists' in the general sense of that term.

> Modernist views may perhaps best be seen as a cluster of positions relating to philosophy, literary analysis, aesthetics and all the social sciences between, very roughly, 1910 and 1970. The views themselves ranged widely in content and application, but they seem united by a particular tone that implied the availability of truth, the undesirability of metaphysics and all forms of blurredness, the necessity for rationalism of an Enlightenment kind.
>
> (Bentley 1997: 487)

In such a climate the excitement of discovery, identification of hidden structures and the digging up of clues bound historians together in a single purpose and understanding of their role. This quest for revealed truth allowed a diversity of political stances to flourish. In the UK, for example, where the momentum of the history profession began to expand rapidly after the mid-1950s, accommodated within the modernist frame was the traditional history practised by G. R. Elton and H. R. Trevor-Roper and the radical work of historical Marxists Christopher Hill, Eric Hobsbawm and E. P. Thompson. Moreover, the studies of such historians won a wide and enthusiastic readership. The lay public was captivated and this, in turn, bolstered the status and esteem in which the academic historian was held (Cannadine 1987: 170–1; Stevenson 1993: 67).

Also part of the 'modernist' harvest was the development of new methods aimed at a better understanding of the structure of social change. The pioneering effort in this regard came from France and was expressed in the methods and interests of French scholars associated with the journal *Annales: économies, sociétés, civilisations* (first published in 1929). Central to the history generated by *Annales* and its adherents was an exploration of the interrelation of geography, anthropology, power relations, temporalities (divided into deep structures, conjunctures and immediate events) and mentalities. Inevitably, perhaps, its influence was uneven and slow to gather pace, the first clear footholds outside France being established in Italy and America from the late 1960s. In the historical communities of Germany and the UK – both intuitively conservative – there was more resistance, although in England the journal *Past and Present*, founded by members of the Communist Party Historians Group in 1952, exerted an influence and offered space to unorthodox themes and treatments: social history; methodological and substantive controversy; the investigation of 'history from below' (Le Goff 1983; Huppert 1997).

Although the historical profession in the West from the 1920s to the 1960s may be described, in retrospect, as 'modernist' in orientation, few outside the ideological centre of Marxism thought much about the theoretical grounding of their work. In the UK, where the empirical tradition had put down especially deep roots, it was 'part of the conservative commitment to realism that theory is unnecessary, epistemology and methodology being largely a matter of common-sense' (Parker 1990: 199–200). Elsewhere, too, 'historians did not believe themselves to be modernists because they rarely believed themselves to be anything worth a label. But their enquiries . . . had the modernist feel for realizable truth and a consistent implication that the past was out there as a visitable place' (Bentley 1997: 488). Nevertheless, even in common-sense England, there were a few working historians of the period sufficiently interested in such ideas to want to explore the theoretical basis of their discipline. Prominent in this genre was Herbert Butterfield's *The Whig Interpretation of History* (1931: 30), a polemical essay which denounced history that 'studies the past with reference to the present'. This was a practice which was 'the source of all sins and sophistries in history'; indeed, it was 'the essence of what we mean by the word "unhistorical"'. Despite its lack of precision, Butterfield's essay exerted a growing influence over academic historians and by the early 1970s the single most common charge being levelled by them against the work of educationists specializing in education was **Whiggish** in just this sense (for example, Stephens 1973: 3). As a consequence, almost all academic historians since Rashdall's time had steered well clear of the history of education, tainted, as it was, by association with the colleges and university departments of education.

If the main thrust of Butterfield's essay is the embodiment of 1930s rationalism it is significant that it was taken most to heart in the 1960s, the decade in which a modernist approach to history reached its apogée. This also helps to explain and place in perspective the development of academic history in Britain and the USA in the 1960s and suggests that there remained a sense of shared craftsmanship and professional identity among historians at a time when conservatives and Marxists seemed fundamentally at odds and when the subject matter of history began to shift decisively away from political and towards social history. To elucidate this point in the English context it is useful to compare two historiographical works of the 1960s championing, respectively, the conservative and radical traditions: Elton's

The Practice of History (1967) and Carr's *What Is History?* (1961). At first sight there seems much more that is separating than uniting in Elton's appeal to traditional empirical method and Carr's radically inclined discussion of causation and progress in history. Yet both shared with Butterfield the sense that the past was indeed a visitable place and that the historian's concern is to reveal and elucidate a true account of historical continuity and change. Never mind that Elton asserted the importance of the full corpus of documentary sources available, the centrality of unpredictable personality in human affairs and the study of history for its own sake, while Carr embraced selection and hindsight, emphasized identification of the broad trajectory of historical events and proposed a social role for the historian in the present. Both remained clear that the role of the historian is to reconstruct the past through the identification of its most significant themes and, by implication, to attune the contemporary reader to its general meaning and significance.

Such was the self-confidence and optimism of academic history in the UK in the expansionary 1950s and 1960s that to those who have followed it has come to seem a 'Golden Age' free from methodological dispute or economic constraint (Cannadine 1987: 170). However, it was altogether too simplistic to assume that the society upon which historians centred their attention was itself stable and homogeneous. In the UK loss of empire was traumatic and posed a multiracial challenge as large numbers of immigrants arrived from the old colonies. In the USA the civil liberties and desegregation movements were exposing deep divisions in society. In continental Europe student unrest centred on Paris threatened to destabilize governments and pointed to an ossified system of higher education unable to resist the mounting pressure to expand and diversify. Over subsequent decades the rapid growth of higher education in most Western countries led to an enlargement and diversification of the history profession. This, in turn, has allowed a multiplicity of specialisms to flourish which more closely reflected the interests of an increasingly heterogeneous and less deferential undergraduate population. Thus, in the English context it had become clear by the mid-1980s that 'if the last 20 years can be summed up in a phrase it must be "the triumph of social history"'. This had 'suffused the majority of history courses, even in the so-called "straight" history departments', and comprised such themes as: industrialization, social structure, social change, urbanization, culture, leisure and the history of mass and popular movements (Bourne 1986: 58). Yet even in these highly favourable circumstances, education remained, in the UK and elsewhere, an underdeveloped theme in academic history and mainstream historians continued to avoid a field tarred with the educationist's brush.

Despite the thematic diversification in academic history widely evident internationally, it was still being complained as late as 1990 that, outside the Marxist tradition, most historians – particularly those in Britain – were innately conservative, wedded to 'realism' and uninterested in the relationship between history and theory (Parker 1990: 199). A decade later, this situation has changed and it is no longer possible for historians to ignore completely the insistent and fundamental challenge to their discipline being mounted by radical social theorists. Emanating from literary theory and from social critiques such as feminism, the 'postmodern' challenge urges historians to renounce their claims to scientific and objective method (especially narrative method) and adopt once more Kant's rejection of a knowable, objective past.

> Some of the more obvious characteristics common among 'postmodern' writers include . . . a concern to 'decentre' and destabilize conventional academic subjects of enquiry; a wish to see canons of orthodoxy in reading and writing give way to plural readings and interpretations; a fascination with text itself and its relation to the reality it purports to represent; a drive to amplify previously unheard voices from un-privileged groups and peoples; a preoccupation with gender as the most immediate generator of underprivileged or unempowered status; a dwelling on power and lack of it as a conditioner of intellectual as much as political configurations within a culture.
>
> (Bentley 1997: 489–90)

In practice most historians remain intuitively cautious in adopting the term 'postmodern' or in attempting to define and evaluate the 'turn' in intellec-tual climate that it is held to represent. First, a majority remain uninterested in theory. Second, they have remained sceptical, a leading historiographer having pointed out succinctly that the concept 'inevitably falls foul of its own principles when they are applied to itself' (Evans 1997: 231). Third, even if historians could not altogether avoid the influence of postmodernism they could argue for a postponement of its detailed consideration on the ground that it was too new a concept to be properly understood; it 'does not yet itself have a historiography: we shall see much more clearly its historical ramifications in thirty or forty years' time' (Bentley 1997: 489).

Perhaps the most widespread influence of the postmodern 'turn' over a largely reluctant historical community has been the widespread and overt assimilation into undergraduate teaching of concepts formerly of interest only to a few philosophers of history: the proper social role of historical knowledge; the nature of knowledge about the past; the competing political and social contexts within which written and oral history is generated; and the uses to which different histories are put in society (Tosh 2000 [1984]: 17–35). In the light of this it is hardly surprising that the history of so per-vasive a social experience as education should have been the subject of intense historiographical conflict over the past 40 years. However, before we examine these conflicts and their implications in detail it is necessary to reflect on the separate development of education as a field of study along-side the discipline of history.

The field of education

Just as the historical treatise is a genre that predates by over two millennia the establishment of an academic discipline of professional historians, so the field of education has had its disquisitions since antiquity. But only in the past 120 years has it become an organized field for research and teaching, entering the universities as a field of enquiry several decades after the arrival of history. In the meantime, pioneering academic historians in Europe had set out from the mid-nineteenth century to professionalize their discipline through an emphasis on 'scientific' method, the creation of a specialist litera-ture and the cultivation of a specific student audience: future statesmen who might look to history for moral exemplars and practical lessons in public affairs (Slee 1988: 344; Howard 1991: 7–8).

By contrast, although the first professors of education in Britain were appointed in 1876 at St Andrews and Edinburgh, there was at that time no clear agreement about the role of education as a subject of study in the uni-versity. Partly this was due to the diversity of the epistemological foun-dations of the emerging field: developmental psychology and experimental pedagogy coupled uncertainly to an older tradition of philosophical think-ing. But there were other differences too. The student audience for education was quasi-professional – trainee teachers – and the nation state was show-ing a growing interest in undertaking research for its own ends. In the UK, for example, a governmental commission of inquiry into popular education during 1858–61 saw the first systematic review on a national scale of pub-licly funded education, there being, as yet, no university-based field of enquiry. In the years immediately following, two further Royal Commis-sions (during 1861–64 and 1864–67, into 'public' and endowed schools respectively) established decisively in the UK the place of the official govern-ment-sponsored enquiry as an engine of social enquiry about education. Moreover, a further three decades were to elapse before the first appoint-ment in England of the first university professor of education (at Durham in 1895) (Gordon 1990).

The parallel but distinctive development during the nineteenth century of the study of history and education had a lasting influence during the twen-tieth century, although the dynamic has varied from country to country (see Figure 3.1). German scholars, most notably Wilhelm Wundt, pioneered many of the techniques that established internationally the scientific basis of educational research during 1880–1900; furthermore, the philosophical strain in German educational enquiry was also strong and this resulted in university departments of prestige and standing. In France a similar pattern emerged. In the USA and the UK, however, the philosophical tradition was weaker and this encouraged a separation between experimental studies and philosophical or historical enquiry, inhibiting the acceptance of the field in the leading universities and ensuring that the history of education came to

1880 to 1900
- empirical studies indebted to developments in natural (rather than social) science;
- emergence of 'experimental pedagogy';
- coexisting older tradition of philosophical and historical enquiry.

1900 to 1930
- flourishing of quantitative research, including statistical analyses;
- burgeoning of empirical studies, including instruction, curriculum, testing, administrative surveys.

1930 to late 1950s
- diminished impetus for strict scientific approach;
- growing influence of progressive movement combining empirical and social/philosophical research.

Late 1950s to late 1970s
- re-emergence of large-scale research assisted by computer analysis;
- questioning of positivist models of research;
- debate about the disciplinary basis of educational studies.

Late 1970s onwards
- shift to anthropological and hermeneutic research methods;
- merging of hard data/scientific research with qualitative methodologies;
- focus on classroom management drawing on eclectic research (de Landsheere 1985: 1588–96).

Figure 3.1 Phases in the international evolution of educational research. *Source*: Adapted from de Landsheere (1985: 1588–96).

be viewed by professional historians as a narrow, instrumental field of little academic merit (Richardson 1999a: 1–3, 15). In part this was because in a country such as the UK most civil servants and statesmen during the period 1850 to 1950 had themselves been educated in a small group of leading private schools and universities where classics and the humanities were powerful. In consequence, policy priorities and the research which supported them centred on a vision of education as an administrative system rather than a scientific or social scientific enterprise. This was as true during the wave of energetic structural reform of 1850–68 as it was during the second and third decades of the twentieth century, when empirical and statistical techniques became dominant internationally in educational research. For this reason it seemed clear to politicians and government officials that the results from studies of human intelligence undertaken by the psychologist Cyril Burt during 1915–27 should be used to buttress a school system reflecting the Platonic social ideal of differentiated gold, silver and copper groups, each afforded its own kind of school and type of curriculum (McCulloch 1995: 117). To this end the by now well established tradition of official, administratively oriented commissions of enquiry was once more deployed in Britain during 1933–38 and 1941–43 to furnish the detailed argument for implementing and sustaining such a tiered system of schooling for the age group 11–15 (Board of Education 1938: 1943).

The impact of these processes on the study of the history of education in Britain was significant. The conservatism of Oxford and Cambridge ensured that education was only grudgingly acknowledged there as a field of study, set firmly in the context of teacher training. This meant that in Britain, unlike in Germany or France, the theme of education failed to gain a foothold in either the history departments or emerging institutes of experimental pedagogy of the most prestigious institutions. Consequently, education conceived as a general field of enquiry flourished more in the newly created universities, where empirical studies would dominate and the history of education would struggle to maintain a presence, even in teacher training. According to the historian Roy Lowe, the effect of these various influences over the history of education was to encourage the development of three distinct genres, none of which was sufficient on its own to establish the field as a powerful intellectual, cultural or political force. The work of the first generation of teacher trainer historians from the 1880s to the 1920s – Robert Quick, John Adamson and Foster Watson – offered accounts which 'glorified the process of teaching, over-emphasised the significance of teachers as transmitters of culture and, by concentrating upon the continuity of educational tradition effectively established a Whig school which took more than fifty years to supplant'. A second group of administrative and legal authors, active from the 1890s to the 1960s – A. F. Leach, Michael Sadler, R. Fitzgibbon Young and G. A. N. Lowndes – all came to the field from administrative or legal backgrounds and 'without exception their interpretations of the development of schooling reflected a wish to vindicate their own life's work'. The third group of authors, more disparate than the other two, were those who since the 1920s have written autobiographical accounts of their lives as education innovators, many of which 'enshrined an idealised image of their earlier endeavours' (Lowe 1983: 50, 51, 53).

In this way Lowe sets out to identify an uncritical 'English tradition' of the history of education which was dominant during the eight decades from the 1880s to the 1950s, laying the foundation for withering criticism of the field from academic historians in the 1960s. In much the same way, Sol Cohen has reconstructed the development of the field in the USA from the beginning of the twentieth century (Cohen 1976). As in the UK, the philosophical and historical strain of American educational studies increasingly played second string to the developing ascendancy of empirical study of the field in the two decades after 1900, while at the same time being too associated with teacher training to take root in the leading academic history departments. With the economic crisis of the 1930s, funding for large-scale scientific studies of education dried up at the same time that education systems in Europe, the Far

East and the Soviet Union fell under totalitarian (fascist or communist) control. In the Anglo-Saxon world and elsewhere – for example, the USA, Australia, the UK and Sweden – educational research as a whole turned from the apparent certainties of a scientific approach to education in the direction of progressive ideas as a bulwark from authoritarianism: it seemed to offer support to democratic politics as well as an attractive 'combination of empirical research and a social and political philosophy merging the free enterprise, liberal spirit with humanistic socialism' (de Landsheere 1985: 1588). The ravages of war interrupted the development of this strain of research, but as early as 1940 the role of education in post-war reconstruction was being actively canvassed in the UK. With the burgeoning of sociological study of education, especially the study of the sources of educational disadvantage, the impetus of educational research in the UK in the 1940s and 1950s led to widespread interest in the development of comprehensive secondary schooling and the dismantling of selective systems of education.

Up to the early 1960s in North America, Britain and Australasia, the effect of these broader trends in educational research on the study of the history of education was to allow a final flourishing of a progressive Whig history in which educationists in each region could portray the history of education unproblematically as a story of continual improvement and refinement led by a partnership between the education profession and the benign nation state. So, in his historiographical retrospective of the English scene, Lowe added to the roll-call of uncritical historians of education some of those authors most popular with teacher training tutors and students in the immediate post-war years, all of whom 'perpetuated the myths which were first elaborated in the early twentieth century': S. J. Curtis, M. E. A. Boultwood, T. L. Jarman, A. D. C. Peterson, H. M. Pollard, H. C. Barnard and H. C. Dent (Lowe 1983: 58). In Australia, New Zealand and Canada the same purposes were apparent, albeit that here a dominant emphasis was on the positive role of education in nation building itself, alongside the political and social advancement that it helped create (see, for example, McCulloch 1986).

In the United States a mixture of the two themes prevailed through the 1940s and 1950s and it was from here that the first tremors were felt of an historiographical earthquake that would engulf English-language history of education. Starting in 1951, the historical studies pursued in the university departments of education and their implicit support for contemporary progressive education policies came under sustained attack from conservative historians. By 1954 historians across the country were beginning to prepare the rout of the old educationist history. It was left to a young Harvard professor, Bernard Bailyn, to launch the main missile in the form of an unrelenting and savage critique of American educational historiography from 1891 to 1960. Bailyn's work reflected and further stimulated a fundamental shift in what the history of education was supposed to be about. He pointed out that despite the large number of books and articles on various aspects of education, the role of education in American history remained obscure. Moreover, he argued, 'We have almost no historical leverage on the problems of American education. The facts, or at least a great quantity of them, are there, but they lie inert, they form no significant pattern' (Bailyn 1960: 4). An important cause of these problems, according to Bailyn, was the 'separateness' of education as a branch of history, 'its detachment from the main stream of historical research, writing and thinking' (p. 5). The history of education had developed as a 'distinct tributary' with the major purpose of celebrating the growth of modern schooling and the rise of a teaching profession. Its isolation from other historians had been self-intensifying, and it 'soon displayed the exaggeration of weakness and extravagance of emphasis that are the typical results of in-breeding' (p. 9). Bailyn argued that it was vital for the history of education to be united with the 'mainstream' of historical research, both to gain greater 'historical leverage' on contemporary educational issues and to investigate the roles and relationships of education in the history of the United States.

From the epicentre of New England the shock waves spread to Canada with the arrival there of Michael Katz in 1966, reached the UK in 1968 when academic historians began publicly to criticize the history of education, before fanning out to Germany, Holland and Italy, and finally arriving in Australia in the late 1970s and New Zealand in the early 1980s (Wilson 1984; McCulloch 1986; McMahon 1996; Richardson 1999a). It may be argued that in the English-speaking world at least, the isolation of the history of education from the mainstream of academic history was now exacting a heavy price on those educationists who had led the endeavour. The fallout from Bailyn's attack was bitterness and disarray among educationists specializing in history in the United States. In Canada, the UK and Australasia the effects were less traumatic, while nevertheless forcing a similar reorientation of the field away from parochial professional concerns in the direction of a more critical attempt to reconstruct the relation of education historically to society as a whole.

All this occurred at a time when educational research more broadly was entering a period of great expansion, fuelled by post-war economic growth, in which large-scale curriculum development programmes and computer-driven data set analysis figured prominently in many countries. In the event, the period during which there was a coincidence of optimism about the power of education to transform society and the large-scale funding of research aimed at bringing it about was relatively brief, roughly from the mid-1950s to the mid-1970s, with the United States leading the way in terms of both scale and methodological innovation. The optimism of that era was checked abruptly in the industrialized Western countries by economic constraint and disillusionment with the ability of educational research, development and reform to secure clear-cut and pervasive social benefits. In its wake, this reassessment of the limits of social research helped to bring about the intellectual 'turn' of 'postmodernism' already referred to, since when a scientific paradigm for educational and other forms of social science research has come under sustained attack. In the world of educational research it has become widely argued that a combination of quantitative and qualitative method is required for research into enduring educational problems to make headway. Furthermore, even as this realignment occurred, there was no let up in 'the "explosion" of knowledge in the physical and social sciences, especially in psychology, linguistics, economics, and sociology', all of which influenced and contributed to the evolution of a pluralistic form of educational research (de Landsheere 1985: 1595).

As was outlined in the previous section, this expansion of knowledge also transformed the academic study of history in the English-speaking world from the late 1950s, largely replacing the mainstream territory developed in the nineteenth century of national political and institutional narrative with an eclectic array of more recent social and economic history, albeit that the principal method of close documentary analysis has continued to hold sway. Taken together, these developments in educational and historical research might have been expected to lead to a highly productive fusion of the two traditions in which historians would tackle afresh educational themes and acknowledge a debt to the insights of educational research, and in which educationists would draw increasingly on the work and methods of social historians to complement their more experimental and empirical fieldwork research.

To a limited extent this has occurred and many of the examples we discuss in detail in Chapter 4 and cite in Chapters 5 and 6 may be regarded as fruits of such a convergence. Much more commonly, however, English-speaking historians and educationists have eschewed a close working relationship or extensive mixing of research methods and techniques. Several general reasons for this may be advanced and each of these will be briefly illustrated in the English context (see also Richardson 1999a, b). First, and perhaps most significant, has been the disdain of academic historians for the Whiggish, uncritical historiography which flourished in the university departments of education in the first half of the twentieth century. In the UK this cast a long shadow over the perceptions of general historians who first ignored the field, then in the late 1960s and early 1970s subjected it to sustained criticism. For a brief period – roughly the decade from 1965 – educationists made a concerted attempt to build bridges, through both historiographical debate and the historical projects they chose to undertake, but by the late 1970s it was becoming clear that this act of rapprochement had created new problems. The redefinition of 'educational studies' in the mid-1960s along disciplinary lines in which history (along with philosophy, psychology and sociology) was accorded the status of a parent discipline had failed in both of its objectives. On the one hand, academic historians repulsed this attempt to win academic respectability within the universities; on the other, teacher trainees complained that such studies were irrelevant to their needs as students.

This episode pointed to two further general reasons why a convergence of historical and educational research has been an uneven and largely elusive goal: professional rivalry and the role of government. In the UK the government in 1964 had backed the 'four disciplines' model of educational studies (Simon 1990: 134) in an attempt to upgrade the standing of education as an undergraduate field of study in comparison to the short, pragmatic college courses of the immediate post-war period. Yet by 1979 this conception of educational studies began to be dismantled as successive governments, Labour and Conservative, sought to redirect teacher training and the research which underpins it away from overtly disciplinary study towards pedagogy and practical experience. This repositioning was motivated by an attempt to assert and demonstrate political control over education in a period of uncertainty and disillusionment, and is a trend which has continued and become increasingly pervasive to the present day.

These developments have reminded both educationists and historians that they serve different student audiences and political masters. The world of education is practical and political in a way that academic history is not. Most education students are undertaking professional training; levels of university staffing in education ultimately are pinned to demographic shifts in the child population; fashion and funding in the academic study of education – equality of opportunity, curriculum, assessment, school effectiveness – are tied to shifting political priorities. In short, the sanctioning of much of educational research and teaching is in a dependent relationship to central government. By contrast, the academic study of history is a relatively small-scale and autonomous activity, well entrenched in the most prestigious universities. It seeks to influence politicians and 'opinion-formers' rather than be influenced by them, for if the discipline is in any sense practical its claim is to offer lessons in statecraft and in the management of social, economic and political change. In such circumstances it is hardly surprising that academic historians have considered there to be much more to lose than gain in developing closer relations with educationists. At the same time, this instinct has been reinforced by a political climate in which educationists have felt compelled to concentrate most of their effort on research into effective learning and professional practice, a process which has all but squeezed out of educational studies any residual tradition of historical and philosophical enquiry.

The history of education

The preceding section has concentrated on the separate and parallel development of history as a discipline and education as a field of study. A question arising from this analysis is the extent to which the historical study of education has, in practice, comprised separate projects tailored to the professional objectives of two separate and rival academic groups: academic historians and educationists specializing in history. Analysis by William Richardson of the English context (1999a, b) suggests that in the Anglophone world as a whole these parallel traditions have shaped strongly the production of historical studies of education, including their subject matter, interpretative conclusions and intended audiences, albeit that most share a common methodology based on documentary and (for more recent periods) oral sources.

The remainder of this chapter sets out to explore the implications of this legacy for contemporary work in the history of education. In this section consideration is given first to the way in which the sharp historiographical exchanges of the past 40 years have shaped the working definitions of education used in historical studies and the range of conceptual frameworks that this has generated for present-day students to choose between and work within. The discussion then moves to an exploration of problems and opportunities that confront the student who wishes to draw on the experience of recent decades when framing a new research project in the field. In the final section the chapter concludes with some working precepts for those interested in attempting to synthesize the best of the historical and educational research traditions into their project planning.

Issues of definition

A process common in the design of most historical research projects is the selection of dates or a period within which to frame a specific study. A discussion of the evolution by historians of definitions of education can be tackled in just this way. As we have already seen, Roy Lowe has briefly surveyed an 'English tradition' of education historiography stretching from the 1890s to the 1950s and his essay includes a series of historiographical statements about the field made by leading authorities over that period. In the process Lowe notes that while these statements were intended to express succinctly the contemporary rationale for the work of each author, with the passing of time they take on a more complex role. Ultimately, each statement can be read on three separate levels. They stand as a record of the intentions of historians of education at the date they were written; second, they can be seen to help to 'determine the interpretations of, and even the major issues investigated by, subsequent historians of education'; and third, in the light of history itself, they take on a value 'as sources in their own right for future historians', so contributing to the kind of historical reconstruction exemplified in the first part of the present chapter (Lowe 1983: 57).

In the text that follows, the judgement has been made that the turning point in twentieth-century educational historiography arrived in the late

1950s. As briefly recounted above, it was in the USA in 1954 that academic historians from leading faculties were first asked by a wealthy charitable foundation to consider as a group the historiography of education. This led to the constitution in May 1956 of a 'Committee on the Role of Education in American History' (Cohen 1976: 299–300). The phrasing was significant, the impact of education on society being stressed in place of the traditional concern of educationists with the impact of society on education. In 1957 the Committee issued a clear statement on this fundamental point: 'we believe that the relationship of society and education is reciprocal and that the impact of education upon society is much less fully studied than the impact of society on education.' Neither was this aphorism merely semantic or one designed solely to create academic demarcation, for the Committee contended that the history of education devised thus far by educationists provided no leverage over contemporary problems: in 1957 'most of the important questions Americans are now asking about the development and impact of education remain unanswered by current historical writing' (quoted in Bailyn 1960: ix, viii).

Here was an overt challenge to that Whiggish tradition of educational history, allied to a celebration of the educational progress, which had been dominant in the English-speaking universities from the turn of the century. Such was the force of the reaction in the direction laid out in the USA by the Ford Foundation Committee that, within a generation, the Whiggish tradition was all but vanquished. It was last publicly defended in principle by William Brickman in 1982 as a working method for university-based academics (as opposed to 'amateur' authors, where it remains a favoured technique, especially in books aimed at the 'alumni' market – see Richardson 2000) but by this date it had already been eclipsed completely in the USA and the UK, while retaining only a diminishing foothold in Australasia (Spaull 1981; McCulloch 1986). In the light of hindsight it is becoming possible to determine a pattern for Anglophone historiography in education during the twentieth century divided into two periods before and after the publication of Bailyn's *Education in the Forming of American Society* (1960) (see Figure 3.2).

The assignment of historical writing about education – or any set of intellectual fashions – into groupings of this kind is an inherently problematic exercise. Yet as it is a widespread device it is important for the historian to be aware of its limitations. In this particular case there are some historical grounds for its use but it is important to note the exact provenance of the various labels used. In the USA Bailyn did not set himself in opposition to a 'Whig' tradition but labelled the dominant form of historiography as 'patristic', comprised of 'dogma' (Bailyn 1960: 8; 1963: 129); it was in the UK in 1982 that Lowe labelled retrospectively the earlier era as 'Whiggish' in an overt attempt to consign it finally to the sphere of intellectual history (Lowe 1983: 49). On the other hand, Bailyn had by 1964 been labelled a 'revisionist' by his detractors (Brickman 1964: 214–15) and, according to J. Donald Wilson (1984: 2), 'by the mid-1970s the terms "moderate revisionists" and

1900 to mid-1960s (and now much less common)
'Classical' historiography in the 'Whiggish' tradition

- Led by educationists specializing in history.
- Celebratory of tradition with a liberal model of gradual progress in education.
- Mainly narrative in form and usually based on published documentary sources.
- Often on a grand scale, spanning several centuries and linked to national history.
- Emphasis on the role of the teacher in transmitting culture.
- Emphasis on the biographies of 'great men'.
- Plotting of precedents for current practice in education.

1960 to early 1980s (and still continuing)
'Revisionism'

1 Moderate revisionism (still continuing)
- Led by academic historians.
- Manifesto published by Bailyn (1960).
- Emphasis on the impact of education on society, with a reciprocal model of influence between them.
- Mainly narrative in form and based on documentary sources (published and unpublished).
- Emphasis on both formal and informal agencies of education.
- Commitment to the delineation of political and social context of educational change.

2 Radical revisionism (influential in the late 1960s and 1970s)
- Led by a mix of academic historians, educationists and sociologists.
- First exemplary monograph published by Katz (1968).
- Interest in the multiple relationships of education (especially its formal agencies) and society.
- Emphasis on the strength of economic and social structures in explaining educational change.
- Strongly influenced by concepts and theories from social science (e.g. Marxism, feminism).
- Often thematic in form and without a central commitment to narrative.

1980s and 1990s (currently ascendant)
'Post-revisionism'

- Led by educationists dissatisfied with classical historiography and both kinds of 'revisionism'.
- Emphasis on the complex, subtle and often contradictory relationship of education and society.
- Interest in drawing on an eclectic array of social science concepts, theories and research methods (e.g. life history, geography, 'race').
- Influenced by postmodernism and allied cultural critiques.
- Concerned with international and cross-national themes.

Figure 3.2 The historiography of education in the English-speaking world during the twentieth century: main waves.

"radical revisionists" came into common use' in North America to designate two separate camps, both of which were influenced by, yet interpreted differently, Bailyn's earlier critique. This, however, is not to imply that these latter terms were current elsewhere; in the UK, for example, there was little historiographical literature anyway and such terms never took hold sufficiently to be applied to home-grown authors. Meanwhile, the term 'post-revisionist' is used here to group together loosely much of the writing of the past two decades.

In addition to pointing to the need for clarity as to whether intellectual labels are historical or ahistorical, such taxonomies raise other questions for the historian. One concerns the extent to which such labels identify primarily genres and research strategies or specific authors. In the analyses of Bailyn and Lowe of American and British historiography respectively, it is maintained that the most important and influential authors of earlier decades are clearly to be associated with a single genre and strategy. Yet the most widespread criticism of Bailyn's essay was that it over-simplified the historiography under attack, and Lowe's critique has not escaped reproach (Cremin 1970; Wilson 1984). This leads to a second question: the extent to which such taxonomies are value neutral or imply a model of historiographical progress and improvement. Certainly those authors concerned to kick over the traces have tended to employ pejorative labels: Bailyn in criticizing the 'evangelists' of earlier decades; Lowe in distancing himself from 'propagandist' predecessors; and, more recently, Barbara Finkelstein (1992b: 263) in condemning Bailyn and Cremin as 'intellectual imperials' whose work, in turn, now needs to be swept away. It is in Finkelstein's method of historiographical reconstruction that the dangers of the genre are perhaps most apparent. She pins a bewildering array of ahistorical labels to past historians of education – ironically so, in view of her commitment to recovering the 'voice' of historical figures. There is also a progressive strain to her story in which the improvement of historiography sits uncomfortably at odds with another strong theme – borrowed from critical theory – that forward moving narratives are an ideological construct.

Thus there are dangers and limitations in defining the shape of historiographical development in the field. What can be said with some confidence is that in the **revisionist** period the question of how education itself is to be defined historically came to the fore as a pressing methodological issue. This was a particular concern of 'moderates' – mainly academic historians – who took up the challenge of studying the impact of education upon society. Prominent among those authorities in America and Britain who tackled this theme in its most influential phase during the 1960s and 1970s were (in the USA) Bernard Bailyn, Lawrence Cremin and Lawrence Stone, and (in the UK) Gillian Sutherland, Asa Briggs and Nicholas Orme. With the exception of Cremin all may be described as mainstream academic historians. In their various works these authors and educationists sympathetic to their approach offered the following definitions of the processes of education in history.

The entire process by which a culture transmits itself across the generations.

(Bailyn 1960: 14)

Histories of education are often mainly concerned with the organisation of schools and colleges and the ideas of reformers, and as such, addressed to educationists rather than the ordinary reader. But, looked at more generally, the history of education is full of incident and interest, touching on all sides of life, on the outlook and interests of all classes of society.

(Simon 1960: 13)

All schemes for education involve some consideration of the surrounding society, its existing structure and how it will – and should – develop. Thus the interaction of educational provision and institutions with patterns of employment, social mobility and political behaviour are fascinatingly complex.

(Sutherland 1969: 3)

The deliberate, systematic, and sustained effort to transmit or evoke knowledge, attitudes, values, skills, and sensibilities, a process that is more limited than what the anthropologist would term enculturation or the sociologist socialization, though obviously inclusive of some of the same elements.

(Cremin 1970: xiii)

Part of the wider study of the history of society, social history broadly interpreted with the politics, the economics and, it is necessary to add, the religion put in.

(Briggs 1972: 5)

Education seen as in and of society concerns not only schools and universities, teachers and pupils, but also all those social institutions which have at different times shaped it, been influenced by it or become enmeshed in it.

(Lawson and Silver 1973: 1)

If we set out to enquire how, in the widest sense, men were *educated* in medieval times, a whole range of possible influences will come to mind, including family life, social conditions, religious ideas and the tasks and preoccupations of adulthood. Learning will thus be seen to include the acquisition of social habits, the appreciation of nature and the mastery of trades, as well as the study of letters in school; while schooling will appear as only one of the strands of education, and one which in any case involved only a minority of people.

(Orme 1973: 1)

The relationship between formal education and other social processes.

(Stone 1974: v)

These working definitions give an indication of the way in which academic historians and educationists picked up the gauntlet thrown down by the Ford Foundation Committee on the Role of Education in American History in 1957. The scope of such work was broad in intention, embracing the themes and techniques of the 'new' social history then under rapid development, open to all periods of history over the past millennium and aimed well beyond the teacher trainee audience to which such accounts had traditionally been directed.

At the time, the flourishing of this new work in the history of education caused excitement and exhilaration. Since the late 1970s, however, the intentions of 'revisionist' authors of educational history have come in for criticism from successors who have attempted to enlarge further the framework within which projects in educational history are undertaken. In particular, the corpus of work generated from the mid-1960s to the close of the 1970s is now criticized by some for being elitist in its themes and concerns, as well as being insufficiently aware of the distinctive educational experience of the two sexes and of minority groups. A response to such criticism would be that, at their broadest and most generous, the formulations of revisionist authors can easily accommodate changing priorities in social history, such as gender and ethnicity. In this light it is interesting to examine the historiographical agendas laid out by three prominent 'moderate revisionists', each of whom was a leading authority in Anglo-American mainstream academic history in the 1960s, 1970s and 1980s.

1 *Bernard Bailyn's* (1960: 156–49, 73–114) *ten themes for a history of pre-Revolutionary American education:*
   literacy, colonial culture, higher education, cultural leadership, apprenticeship, ethnic difference, denominationalism, the changing role of the state, finance, the family.
2 *Lawrence Stone's* (1969: 69–98) *seven dimensions for the historical study of education:*
   the labour market, resources, demographic patterns, social stratification, theories of social control, institutions, political theory.
3 *Asa Briggs's* (1972: 5–22) *seven aspects of the history of education:*
   local, comparative, quantitative, social, political, intellectual and cultural.

Taken together, these three agendas, formulated during 1960–72, are sufficiently broad in their scope to embrace almost all of the history of education that has been written since. Indeed, most of the criticism of revisionism by 'post-revisionist' authors is directed not so much at the scope of the studies proposed but at the interpretations offered. In this way Bailyn – perhaps the most conservative of the three authors cited here – has been damned by Finkelstein for having 'located the history of education in the history of ideas', especially the civic tradition extolled by the nation state. For her, this approach was crucially flawed, being a form of reconstruction which 'relegated power struggles and conflict to a kind of theoretical backseat', so denying their role as a 'reasonable explanation of change' (Finkelstein 1992b: 263, 265–6). But this tells us more about Finkelstein's interpretative preoccupations than the sagacity of Bailyn's framing of the historiographical field. Perhaps more problematic is the extent to which it is possible or desirable to conflate the historiographical agenda of the revisionist approach to education so as to create a new synthesis or 'metanarrative' to replace those of the period of classical, Whiggish historiography of education of 1900–60. The one author who has attempted this on the grand scale for four centuries of American education is Lawrence Cremin (1970, 1980, 1988), and while almost all critics have admired the scope, ambition and industry of Cremin's work, most have concluded that the task begs at least as many questions as it answers (see *History of Education Quarterly* 1989: 419–46).

So, while the redefinition of the scope of the field opened up by the process of revisionism in the 1960s and 1970s has retained its significance to the present, the interpretative options within this frame continue to generate controversy and debate. This is especially the case when the concepts, theories and techniques of social science are brought to bear on the educational past (as anticipated, in particular, by Lawrence Stone), and this is a subject to which we turn in more detail in the next chapter. At this point we might summarize by saying that of the two challenges posed by the Ford Foundation Committee in 1957 – the need to reconstruct the impact of education on society and to examine the reciprocal nature of each upon the other – 'revisionist' and 'post-revisionist' historians of education have found it easier to agree on ways of tackling the first but continue to disagree widely over the methods appropriate to the second.

History and education: what kind of convergence?

The main result of the clash between the 'moderate' and 'radical' revisionists of the 1960s and 1970s has not been a reorientation in any particular direction in the 'post-revisionist' phase of the past 20 years, but the assimilation into historical studies of education of an eclectic array of research methods and concepts. While the traditional historical monograph survives in the form exemplified by the moderate revisionists, more common latterly has been an approach to the historical study of education which draws freely, even opportunistically, from a range of theories, constructs and present concerns in social science and cultural studies. Under such conditions an American authority has warned that 'because no new methodological or ideological consensus has emerged – in short, because there is no successful paradigm in educational history today – it is all the more important that each reader of educational history be critically alert and independent' (Kaestle 1988: 71).

Kaestle might equally have applied this stricture to the authors of such studies for, as we have suggested in this chapter and in Chapter 2, they are now, more than ever before, aware of the choices in methodology and interpretative frame available and the opportunity they offer. In turn, this implies that a convergence between the kind of educational history championed by a moderate revisionist such as Bernard Bailyn and a radical such as Michael Katz is now well under way, supplemented by studies of the recent past which owe more to the fieldwork techniques and theoretical concerns of 'social research' than traditional historical method. In retrospect this set of developments may be seen as almost inevitable. Younger historians formed in the period of ferment and controversy came to maturity in different ways. Within academic history there has been increasing openness to the value of social theory in the setting of research questions in history; only for the staunchest conservative – in the UK, G. R. Elton, for example – has this prospect been resisted as fraught with danger. Meanwhile, educationists trained as historians have found themselves marginalized as educational studies has become more and more **present-minded**. The response of many such survivors has been to trim hard and turn towards social science methodology.

Central to this developing convergence has been an accommodation between history on the one hand and a combination of sociology and anthropology on the other, a theme explored more fully in the next chapter. Moreover, the present-day student is at a considerable advantage compared to the situation of a generation ago. The decade from the mid-1960s was characterized, in the UK at least, by a debate about the potential for fusion of history with sociology that remained exploratory and inconclusive (Chaloner and Richardson 1984: 1–5). By the mid-1970s this debate was coming to life in the field of educational history, especially in the United States, where historiographical concerns were openly explored, through the exemplary monographs and edited texts of moderate revisionists such as Cremin, Sol Cohen and J. Axtell, radicals such as Katz, Clarence Karier and Joel Spring and a figure such as David Tyack, who attempted to steer a middle course between them (Cohen 1976). In the UK, a similar separation was apparent in the work of moderates such as Keith Thomas (1976) – although like Bailyn, influenced by anthropology – and radicals such as Richard Johnson (1970). Meanwhile, in mid-Atlantic, as it were, Lawrence

Stone (1969: 69) was sending dispatches from his 'trial balloon' named *History of Education*, blowing on the winds and currents between the two physical and historiographical continents. In Canada, and later in Australasia, there was a similar development of rival moderate and radical interpretative frames (Richardson, 1999a, b).

By the mid-1980s and thereafter, as the younger, 'post-revisionist' historians of education began to make an impression in the USA, as a new generation of academic historians began to be appointed in Britain after the retrenchment of 1981–86 eased, as the combined influence of 'postmodernism' and right-leaning government began to be felt in both history and education, and as the number of educationists specializing in history began to fall away as educational studies became ever more focused on field-based social science, the dichotomy of moderate and radical social and educational history began to break down. In the UK in 1986 Keith Thomas used a Royal Historical Society lecture on the history of numeracy to berate gently 'those historians who do not regard their discipline as a form of retrospective ethnography' (Thomas 1987: 103); meanwhile, although Geoffrey Elton continued to carry the conservative banner new recruits were in decreasing supply. In Australasia, where the spirit of revisionism in educational history was only now gathering strength, it arrived late enough to be assimilated by a fresh generation of academic historians formed in a milieu infused with feminism and postmodernism. In the USA it could be said of educational history in 1988 that 'the excitement of the last 20 years has not resulted in a single new methodology, nor in a broadly accepted interpretation of educational history'. Instead, the order of the day was – then and since – for historians of education to 'discard old assumptions, try new techniques, and attempt to meet more rigorous standards of evidence and argument' (Kaestle 1988: 67). For some in the university departments of education, such as Finkelstein (1992b: 274), this meant an inevitable radicalization as, in the face of 'overwhelming professional and political pressures', they set about using the history of education to fuel current debates in social and cultural studies by seeking out lost oppositional voices from the past, especially those which might illustrate the structuring of society through the concepts of race, class, gender and public authority (Finkelstein 1992b: 275–83).

Thus the present situation is one in which the history of education is more open than ever before to a creative relationship between the traditional strengths of history and the empirical social sciences. Potentially, this milieu allows historians to draw on an increasing range of tools with which to recover, reconstruct and interpret the complex relation of education and society and the reciprocal influence of each upon the other. Increasingly, this mediating, problematic, dynamic relationship is central to historical studies of education in stark contrast to the situation of a generation ago. As such, researchers need, as a minimum, to be fully familiar with the concerns and methods of research in history and in the social sciences as applied to education (Ringer 1977). Moreover, there is the potential to undertake historical study of themes amenable to this multidisciplinary approach which are also highly topical in education across the English-speaking world – themes such as curriculum, the gendered experience of education (including attainment), urban education, education policy and the nature of teaching.

In the process, working in topical fields with complex sources of evidence should encourage authors, especially educationists, to think more clearly about the nature and interests of their audience. This is a theme to which we return in Chapters 5 and 6 but, for now, it may be noted that in general terms some research methods are especially helpful for synthesizing the two research traditions which have been the subject of this chapter. For example, there are methods usually associated with the historical tradition – especially unpublished documents in archives – which have, on the whole, been underutilized in educational research. Conversely, some methods usually associated with educational research – most notably interview technique – have been neglected in contemporary history.

In this chapter and in Chapter 2 we have deliberately contrasted the traditions of history as a discipline and education as an applied field drawing mainly on social science in order to clarify important strands in the development of each. We have argued that for most of the twentieth century it is their distinctiveness which has influenced the conception and practice of rival kinds of historical study of education. Towards the end of this chapter we have suggested that these separate traditions are now in the process of breaking down and converging, and that this offers considerable potential for helping historians of education with their most complex task – that of understanding the reciprocal relation of education and society in different places and in different eras. A most eloquent invocation of the possibilities offered by this kind of synthesis is offered by John Tosh:

> history cannot be defined as either a humanity or a social science without denying a large part of its nature. The mistake that is so often made is to insist that history be categorised as one to the exclusion of the other. History is a hybrid discipline which owes its endless fascination and its complexity to the fact that it straddles the two. If the study of history is to retain its full vitality, this central ambivalence must continue to be recognised, whatever the cost in logical coherence. The study of history 'for its own sake' is not mere antiquarianism. Our human awareness is enhanced by the contemplation of vanished eras, and historical re-creation will always exercise a hold over the imagination, offering as it does vicarious experience to the writer and reader alike. At the same time, historians also have a more practical role to perform, and the history which they teach, whether to students in schools and colleges or through the media to the wider public, needs to be informed by an awareness of this role. In this way a historical education achieves

a number of goals at once: it trains the mind, enlarges the sympathies *and* provides a much-needed historical perspective on some of the most pressing problems of our time.

(Tosh 2000 [1984]: 34–5)

In this spirit, we now turn to a consideration of the role of the insights of specific social sciences in the recreation of the educational past.

4 | The challenge of the social sciences

In this chapter, we examine how a range of different social sciences, especially sociology but also psychology, economics, geography, cultural studies and anthropology, have been applied to historical research in education, and the issues that are involved. This is a highly important strand in the development of the field. The social sciences have greatly extended it theoretically and methodologically, and have fostered many significant interdisciplinary connections. Their prominent role means that the history of education has become integrated with the social sciences no less than it is with the humanities. In addition, the interdisciplinary character of the research that such social science applications encourage has served to erode the rigid demarcation between 'education' and 'history' evident in the English-speaking world during most of the twentieth century. Inevitably, however, the application of concepts and methodologies from the social sciences also brings with it characteristic dilemmas of which the researcher needs to be aware.

The social science discipline that has been especially influential in historical research in education is sociology. Here we recognize the extent of that contribution by examining the character of its development and providing a range of examples, especially those which illustrate the concepts that have been applied to education in a historical perspective. Several other social science disciplines have also made significant inroads into the field, and we discuss the contribution each has made, while attempting also to highlight the essentially interdisciplinary nature of much of this work.

Sociological imaginations

There is a very large body of literature that attempts to relate sociological theory and methodology to historical research in the area of education, reflecting the close relationship that has developed especially since the 1960s between social history and sociology. In the past, sociology has been dismissed by many historians as being politically subversive, obscure in style and either too theoretical or naively empirical. For their part, sociologists have often been impatient with the narrow, non-scientific, descriptive, elite-oriented cast of much historical writing. As Burke (1980: 14) has noted, 'Sociologists seem to think of history as if it were still in the Ranke phase of narrative without analysis; historians seem to think of sociology as if it were still in the Comte phase of grand generalisations without empirical research.' Nevertheless, what has often been called a **historical sociology** has latterly developed through the joint enterprise of many historians and sociologists.

Over the past 35 years historians in many countries have become increasingly interested in social change as experienced by different groups and individuals in society, and so have come to employ a range of sociological devices and concepts to enlarge their historical accounts. In the 1960s and 1970s, leading social historians such as Plumb and Briggs in Britain and Hofstadter in the United States endorsed a general lowering of the barriers between history and sociology (Briggs 1967; Hofstadter 1968; Plumb 1982). Equally, many sociologists in the same period took up the famous declaration of C. Wright Mills in *The Sociological Imagination* that 'All sociology worthy of the name is "historical sociology"' (Mills 1959: 146). Abrams, for example, perceived a dramatically narrowing gap between the two disciplines. Sociologists and historians, he argued, were equally concerned with 'the puzzle of human agency', and sought to understand it 'in terms of social structuring' (Abrams 1982: x). Indeed, according to Abrams, there was no necessary difference in intention between the sociologist and the historian, since any sociology that takes itself seriously must be 'historical sociology'; that is, 'the attempt to understand the relationship of personal activity and experience on the one hand and social organisation on the other as something that is continuously constructed in time' (p. 16).

The precise terms of this alliance and the different roles of the partners have continued to cause some dispute. For example, Tilly (1981: 12) has insisted that there can be no simple 'disciplinary division of labour' between 'transcribing' historians and 'analytical' sociologists. Explicit theory should be regarded as being just as important for historians as for sociologists. In other words, both in their different ways should be 'searching for theories that have adequate historical grounding', sensitized to different problems and opportunities by training and experience (pp. 213–14). This theme has also been pursued by Gareth Stedman Jones, who rejects any notion of demarcation lines between 'empirical' history and 'theoretical' sociology in favour of a 'theoretical history' in which historians will themselves engage in critical theory (Stedman Jones 1976; also 1982: Chapter 2). In complementary vein, Banks (1989) considers historical sociology to be an 'essential research technique' for sociologists when they are attempting to 'differentiate between what persists and what changes in social relationships over varying amounts of time' (p. 540), and that this in turn entails careful analysis of documentary and contemporary evidence. Conversely, other sociologists have continued to emphasize that history and sociology should be treated as 'significantly different intellectual enterprises' – for example, due to the nature of the evidence that they employ (Goldthorpe 1991: 225) – while some historians have remained uncompromising in their overall suspicion of social theory (Elton 1991: 3–26).

However, there has been a general convergence between history and sociology which has been vividly reflected in the field of education. In the 1960s and 1970s there were several explicit and elaborate attempts to integrate historical and sociological approaches to the study of education. For instance, the 'new sociology' of education developed at that time sought both social and historical explanations for 'what counts as knowledge' in modern societies (Young 1971). 'Perhaps it is not too much to hope', suggested Gerald Bernbaum, 'that those who work in the field of education, with its wide-ranging perspectives and tradition of inter-disciplinary activity, might pioneer historical sociology in order that we might better understand not only the educational system, but also the educational process' (Bernbaum 1971: 18). Other proselytizers of such an outlook in the British context have included Szreter (1969), Musgrave (1970) and Warwick and Williams (1980).

Unfortunately, sociological work in this area has not always displayed sophistication, especially where it appears that history is being used without sufficient attention to changing contexts. Silver, for example, has referred to a characteristic tendency to 'raid the past' or adopt a selective use of history in the search for telling examples to support a particular theme (Silver 1980: 279). In some cases, too, the sociological theory fits uneasily with the historical evidence that is brought to bear upon a problem. Problems often arise where a theory developed in one cultural or national context is applied to fit a different culture or nation. **Anachronisms** are common in cases where explanations of a long-term trend are made in terms that would only make sense for a short-term or contemporary case. There are also methodological and ethical dimensions to these issues; for example, whereas ethnographic accounts of schools have avoided identifying the institution and individuals involved (see Hargreaves 1967; Lacey 1970; Ball 1981), most historical and biographical work emphasizes the importance of establishing details of identity and context. Thus, even though differences can be exaggerated, tensions remain between the sociological exploration of theoretical models, and the historical endeavour to understand particular experiences in their context. Nevertheless, a substantial and indeed highly influential literature that may be described as 'historical sociology' has been established in the field of education, and has continued to develop over the past two decades, although there are major and surprising gaps in this literature. For example, there have been few explicit or sustained attempts to relate the important sociological studies of Basil Bernstein on class and forms of pedagogy to a historical framework or analysis, although Goodson (1995) has noted Bernstein's influence on his approach to curriculum history (see also Grace 1995). Bernstein himself notes that it would be interesting to discover where and when what he terms 'invisible pedagogy' first entered the secondary school curriculum, and suggests that in Britain it may first have penetrated the 'non-verbal' areas of unselective secondary schools such as the area of the art room (Bernstein 1997: 73–4).

Much of the most important sociological theory informing historical research in the area of education has been developed in continental Europe, and especially in France. The classic work of Emile Durkheim, both professor of pedagogy and sociologist, at the beginning of the twentieth century helped to establish this tradition. Durkheim adopted a systematic and historical approach to explore the structure and process of educational transmission; for example, in his work *The Evolution of Educational Thought* (1904). What is more, over 70 years later it was being suggested that 'No sociologist of education has yet surpassed – in depth or in breadth – this investigation of the relationship between social structure and educational transmission' (Karabel and Halsey 1977: 74).

More recently, intellectuals of the calibre of Louis Althusser, Pierre Bourdieu and Michel Foucault have maintained this strong French tradition by emphasizing the social relationships within education and how these are in a dynamic with changing contemporary concerns. Althusser, a prominent neo-Marxist theorist, described schools as 'ideological state apparatuses' that were designed by their very nature to perpetuate capitalist 'hegemony', or cultural domination (Althusser 1972). Bourdieu's work has set out to explore how education contributes to social reproduction, highlighting a process which he labelled the 'cultural capital' stored by middle-class families and pupils (Bourdieu and Passeron 1977; see also Grenfell and James 1998). The account developed by Foucault of the disciplinary nature of modern social institutions, including schools just as much as hospitals and prisons, has also raised profound issues for historians of education to pursue (Ball 1990; see also the case study of Foucault and educational history towards the end of this chapter). Educational history in France in particular has drawn not only on these sociological insights, but on the pervasive influence of Fernand Braudel and his 'Annales' school of historians, and been applied in a country where traditionally there has been a strong emphasis on the social and political importance of education (for example, Baker and Harrigan 1980; Mayeur 1984).

Bourdieu's theories of 'social reproduction' and 'cultural capital' have also been deployed in historical research further afield to inform an understanding of educational and social inequalities. From this perspective Teese (1995: 357), in an examination of private and public schooling in Australia after the Second World War, suggests that:

Between the family, with its 'cultural capital', and the curriculum, with the social assets which it contained, came the mediating role of the school . . . The transformation of intellectual debt into scholastic equity underlies many of the processes through which schools exploited their social intake: selection and promotions policies, subject offerings and streams, instructional strategies, extra-curricular activities, organisational structures. But the effectiveness of these processes depended on where a school was located within the social and institutional geography of the school system.

He supports this thesis through an investigation of the curriculum in different schools in the state of Victoria in the mid-1970s, and concludes that the advantages of the private schools over the public high schools were maintained during this period 'not only by the resources which each new cohort of private school users could mobilise to achieve a contemporary advantage, but by the historical resources conserved in the curriculum which made learning its own virtue and knowledge a point of culture, not application' (Teese 1995: 367).

Similarly, Ringer (1987) has drawn on the potential uses of Bourdieu's ideas. As national education systems become more complex they 'come to play', he argues, 'more central roles in perpetuating social hierarchies, and it is this development we have tried to understand under the heading of education and social reproduction' (Ringer 1987: 5). At the same time, however, Ringer is conscious of the limitations of Bourdieu's model. In particular, he suggests, it is 'rather **unhistorical**', in that the processes involved in his depiction of the education system seem 'timelessly and almost too perfectly to fulfil its reproductive function'. According to Ringer (1987: 5), therefore, there is a need for a more contextually nuanced account:

I suspect that the degree of separation or incongruity between the distributions of economic and cultural capital has varied historically and from country to country, that it was greater during the early nineteenth century than it is today, and that it has in fact been attenuated by the convergence between education and occupation since about 1870.

Moreover, Ringer adds, although Bourdieu's conception of cultural and social reproduction is 'indispensable for the social historian of education and of knowledge', his understanding of 'cultural capital' is 'not explicitly and fully enough linked to the past . . . Here again, Bourdieu might give more attention to genuine change over time, to historical contingency and variability, and thereby also to the social and ideological incongruities induced by the presence of the past' (p. 10). Thus, Ringer uses Bourdieu's ideas as an important starting point for his historical research, but is critical of their explanatory power in relation to different societies and historical contexts. Such critical engagement with theory, as opposed to an uncritical application of theory, can be an important asset for the historical researcher in the field of education. How to understand this engagement, and how to carry it out in practice, are key facets of the challenge of the social sciences to which we return in Chapter 7.

Education and the social order

Controversies over the role of theory in historical writing about education have not, of course, taken place in a vacuum. Indeed, much of the momentum for such debates has arisen from the work of sociologists of education engaged in research on contemporary questions who have, for a variety of reasons, found it useful to explore the historical record as part of their analysis. We now illustrate this process through an account of prominent postwar studies of education, from Britain in the main, in which sociologists and other social researchers have adopted a historical perspective in their work or sought to explore the extent to which social theory is supported by historical evidence. The account is organized in two parts: studies on education and social change undertaken from the 1940s to the 1970s; and studies concerned with policy, gender and comparative analysis of education systems carried out over the past 30 years.

Education and social change

In Britain, as elsewhere, a great deal of sociological research since the Second World War has sought to document the relationship between education and social class. Fred Clarke's influential work *Education And Social Change*, published in 1940, adopted the 'sociological standpoint' and sought to explore 'its concrete application to the field of English education' (Clarke 1940: 1). This task, as Clarke saw it, required him

> to attempt an interpretation, conscious and deliberate, in terms of a social economic history, and then, in the light of that interpretation, to estimate the capacity of the English educational tradition to adapt itself without undue friction or shattering to the demands of a changed order.
> (Clarke 1940: 1)

Many of the key dimensions of the English educational tradition that were usually taken for granted, according to Clarke, were sociological rather than educational in nature, and he traced their 'historical determinants' in order to demonstrate this. The ideas of the sociologist Karl Mannheim were also highly influential in helping to appraise the social characteristics of educational institutions at this time (Taylor 1996).

Picking up Clarke's theme, some important sociological research was undertaken in Britain in the 1950s to investigate the social effects of the

Education Act of 1944, and, in particular, the extent to which it had enhanced social mobility. David Glass, a leading sociologist, suggested that the 1944 Act was potentially the most important measure of the past half-century for the dismantling of social stratification (Glass 1954: 4). This led him to stress in particular the social inequalities that remained, first owing to leaving independent boarding schools (or 'public schools') outside the state system of education, and second because of the development of a 'tripartite system' of secondary schools (grammar, technical and modern). Other researchers found detailed evidence both of social inequality and of opportunities for social mobility (for example, Floud 1954; Himmelweit 1954). An extended work produced by Olive Banks (1955) also demonstrated the ambiguous nature of the changes that had been made, especially in relation to the failure of reforms in secondary education to achieve 'parity of esteem' between different types of school and forms of knowledge. Taking a more overtly historical stance, Banks examined the influence of the idea of the grammar school on the different forms of secondary education that had been developed since the Education Act of 1902, and followed a chronological sequence in doing so. However, she emphasized, her study was not intended to constitute a history of the public system of secondary education, and indeed her notion of 'secondary education' was somewhat anachronistic in relation to the period 1902–44. Rather, Banks observed, she wished to explore 'those events, and in particular those controversies, which shed the most light on the social function of the various forms of secondary education, and on the sociological implications of the development of the secondary grammar school' (Banks 1955: 12). She concluded that the history of English secondary education had been powerfully influenced by its role in selection for social mobility, and that this in turn had been shaped by the requirements of different kinds of occupations: 'The movement towards educational equality is thus seen, in the last resort, to be dependent on the wider social movements of our time' (Banks 1955: 248).

The relationship between education and these wider social movements was tellingly satirized later in the decade by another leading British sociologist, Michael Young, in his *The Rise of the Meritocracy* (1958). This extraordinary work, which coined the term 'meritocracy' that was quickly to enter the language, is based in the year 2033 and develops a historical analysis beginning from the Elementary Education Act of 1870 to explain Britain's development from being the 'workshop of the world' in the nineteenth century, to becoming the 'grammar school of the world' in the twenty-first century. This trend had been made possible, he suggested, partly through the spread of grammar schools for the academic elite, and the emulation that they encouraged, but also because of the victory of the principle of 'merit', ascertained by regular competitive examination, which overrode earlier principles of selection, such as birth, wealth and length of service. It is a social movement that ends in revolution as the socially inferior, dispossessed and alienated, because of their lack of merit, rise up against their new masters.

The sociological literature of this period, including Young's history of the future, effectively established the dominant tone of critical perspectives on education in Britain, based mainly on social class differences and inequalities. This was again evident in Raymond Williams's classic, if brief, historical treatment of education and British society, published in 1961. Education, according to Williams, expressed both consciously and unconsciously 'the wider organization of a culture and a society', in such a way that 'what has been thought of as simple distribution is in fact an active shaping to particular social ends' (p. 125). The content or curriculum of education was bound up with cultural and social choices, and therefore in order to understand education at all adequately it was essential to 'examine, in historical and analytical terms, this organic relation'. In particular, he identified three distinct and often contradictory social purposes underlying education: training for a vocation, training to a social character and training a particular civilization, which were championed by 'industrial trainers', 'public educators' and 'old humanists', respectively. He examined the history of English education since the sixth century AD to demonstrate the relationships between these aims in a changing social context. The school curriculum, he suggested, represented what he called 'a compromise between an inherited selection of interests and the emphasis of new interests' (p. 150). Indeed, he added,

> At varying points in history, even this compromise may be long delayed, and it will often be muddled. The fact about our present curriculum is that it was essentially created by the nineteenth century, following some eighteenth-century models, and retaining elements of the medieval curriculum near its centre.
>
> (Williams 1961: 150–1)

Williams emphasized the pervasive influence of social class thinking on educational debate since the nineteenth century, and concluded, somewhat predictably, that social and cultural tensions were an ever-present feature of education and remained unresolved and contested in contemporary society.

Perhaps the most influential of the British sociologists with regard to understanding the history of education has been A. H. Halsey. No less concerned than other sociologists of his generation with the relationships between education and social class, he built up a considerable array of empirical data designed to identify the nature of the social influence of education over the generations. His early research helped to establish the predominantly middle-class character of grammar schools as distinct from the mainly working-class population of secondary modern schools (for example, Halsey and Gardner 1953). He then proceeded to develop a comprehensive analysis of the nature and extent of social mobility in twentieth-century

Britain that emphasized the central importance of educational institutions, including the family, as 'an active agent of cultural evolution and social selection' (Halsey 1978: 111). This research culminated in 1980 in the publication of *Origins and Destinations*, a detailed survey of the relationships between family, class and education in modern Britain. *Origins and Destinations* was based principally on a survey of 8,529 men aged between 20 and 64 living in England and Wales who were asked in 1972 about aspects of their life histories. Its conclusions helped to answer the questions raised by sociologists in the 1950s, from the perspective allowed a quarter of a century later, especially in its declaration that 'the 1944 Education Act brought England and Wales no nearer to the ideal of a meritocratic society' (Halsey *et al.* 1980: 210). However, the use of the term 'meritocratic society' in this context might itself be considered problematic. As we have seen, Young invented the word 'meritocracy' only in 1958, and had a very different view of its social effects, which suggests that even well respected and experienced sociologists such as Halsey can be guilty of anachronism or distortion.

The questions and frameworks established by these sociologists, especially their emphasis on the relationship between education and social class, has also shaped the concerns of many historians of education from the 1960s through to the end of the twentieth century. Simon's work (1960), which led the way in this regard in Britain, was built around the idea of 'two nations', defined in terms of social class, and their relationship to the structure of educational provision, while Silver (1973: viii–xi) declared not only that the 'outstanding feature' of nineteenth-century educational history in Britain was the conscious establishment of two separate educational systems, but also that discussion of education and social class had been 'the most prolonged educational issue of twentieth-century Britain'. Meanwhile, the radical historical revisionism that developed in the United States in the late 1960s reinforced a tendency already apparent in Britain, with the result that social class has continued to be a principal concern for English-speaking historians of education in subsequent decades, expressed in various ways.

In the 1970s in particular, applications of social class theory were highly fashionable as devices to help to interpret the history of mass schooling in Britain. Richard Johnson led the way in elaborating the role of 'social control' as a motive for middle-class support of working-class schooling in the nineteenth century (Johnson 1970; see also, for example, Donajgrodski 1977). On this view, middle-class advocacy for educating the working class, relatively weak though such advocacy was in England in the first half of the century, was to be explained principally in terms of the aim of controlling an unruly and potentially dangerous newly industrialized populace, and also to maximize economic productivity (see also Kaestle 1976). The idea of 'socialization' was also applied in an attempt to understand how nineteenth-century elementary schools and other kinds of institutions had transmitted skills, values and social norms to working-class pupils (McCann 1977).

The writings of the political economists Samuel Bowles and Herbert Gintis, especially their major work *Schooling in Capitalist America* (1976), also influenced research in the history of education. Bowles and Gintis argued that the principal effect of unequal schooling was to reproduce the social division of labour between the owners and producers of capital. Indeed, they proposed, there was a clear and direct correspondence between the social organization of schooling and that of work. In Part III of their study, on the dynamics of educational change, they focused on the historical development of schools and higher education to help to explain the nature of this correspondence. Chapter 6, for example, explored the origins of mass public education in the United States. This revealed, they suggested, 'not a smooth adjustment of educational structure to the evolution of economic life, but rather a jarring and conflict-ridden course of struggle and accommodation' (Bowles and Gintis 1976: 151). This, it appeared to them, reflected the impact of schooling on consciousness, ideology and the social class structure, and laid bare major discrepancies between the rhetoric and reality of educational reform. Thus, they announced, 'There can be little doubt that educational reform and expansion in the nineteenth century was associated with the growing ascendancy of the capitalist mode of production' (Bowles and Gintis 1976: 178). During the twentieth century, too, according to Bowles and Gintis, 'the role of education in capitalist expansion and the integration of new workers into the wage-labor system came to dominate the potential role of schooling as the great equaliser and the instrument of full human development' (Bowles and Gintis 1976: 181). Their historical account matched up with and helped to reinforce the radical revisionism of American historians such as Michael Katz in a process which advanced more strongly than before interpretations of educational history that were based on social theory rather than supported by it. Moreover, as a working model their correspondence theory encapsulated the dominant concern with social class that had been generated within sociology, and with it the increasingly deterministic and structural nature of 'social control'. These tendencies were soon to be challenged, both by historians and from within sociology itself.

Policy, gender and comparative models

Continued sociological interest in the development of state schooling in Britain was vividly reflected in the publication of *Unpopular Education* (CCCS 1981), an extended polemical treatment of the development of the education system since the Education Act of 1944. This work, although historical in nature, was strongly influenced by contemporary social, economic and political developments in Britain, especially the end of post-war consensus around the welfare state, the growth of unemployment, the perception of long-term relative economic and industrial decline and the emergence of aggressive right-wing policies that were soon to become labelled those of the 'New Right'. Margaret Thatcher's Conservative government was elected to office in 1979, signalling the beginning of an 18-year period of Conservative rule during which education became increasingly the target for radical reform. *Unpopular Education*, produced by the Education Group at the Centre for Contemporary Cultural Studies (CCCS), whose leading light was Richard Johnson, attempted to explain the apparent failure of Labour Party policies on education since the 1940s which had allowed the Conservative Party to regain the initiative in this area during the late 1970s. It argued that

> The failure of the Labour Party to muster more than a minimal opposition either to the challenge to or subsequent dismantling of the post-1944 consensus has dramatically confirmed our major theses – that the old repertoire of Labour Party policies is largely exhausted in the forms in which it is currently conceived and presented.
>
> (CCCS 1981: 7)

It developed this argument mainly through the conceptual device of 'education settlements'. This proposed that consensus or settlement around specific policies tended to be achieved through compromise that concealed inherent contradictions. These contradictions in turn led to the breakdown of the settlement, or a crisis, and a search for a new basis for consensus. It was a Marxist analysis that steered away from the earlier determinist and structural accounts of 'social control' (mainly also Marxist in inspiration) and towards notions of a dialectic of resistance and active opposition to class or cultural hegemony.

According to *Unpopular Education*, the settlement around the Education Act of 1944, which had been a cross-party measure, gave way to a new settlement in the 1960s that was more radical and socialist in nature but was not fully followed through. This was now being undermined and replaced by a Conservative-based consensus that stressed the need to promote educational standards and economic productivity, rather than social equality and justice. Not all educational historians were convinced by this account. For example, Silver was prompted to launch a powerful criticism of this kind of use of 'strong theory', arguing that it was concerned more with developing theory than with the history itself, and that this led it into errors and distortions. According to Silver, 'The central weakness of the book, in fact, is its struggle to escape from an inhibiting and frustrating theory . . . [and] its willingness to remain within that theory, and to parade the history like the captions on archaeological exhibits – produced as shorthand guides to an already established collection' (Silver 1981: 296; see also the reply to Silver's criticism by Baron *et al.* 1982, and further discussion of the controversy in Silver 1983). However, it was plausible enough for other sociologists to take up and develop further to explain contemporary changes in education policy both in Britain and elsewhere. Grace, for instance, applied this model first to help to understand the changing relationship of teachers with the state in Britain since the 1940s (Grace 1987) and then to appraise debates around education policy in New Zealand (Grace 1991). More broadly, the rapidly changing educational policy scene and the social and political antagonisms that it reflected came to attract strong sociological interest that often included interpretation of the historical developments involved over the longer term (for example, Chitty 1989; Dale 1989; Johnson 1989). It was again Silver who reflected on the implications of this growth area for historical research, expressing concern over the tensions between history and theory and the problems involved in anachronism. Even so, he concluded that in finding a legitimate role for themselves, 'historians will be inevitably and usefully compelled to review their own organizing concepts and assumptions, to learn from evaluators, ethnographers and others grappling from different directions with the same complex sequences and processes' (Silver 1990: 30).

Also by the 1980s, feminist sociologists from a range of parallel perspectives (see, for example, Weiner 1994) made a determined attempt internationally to challenge the social class orientation and the predominantly male-centred focus of historical research on education. In the USA Burstyn complained in 1977 that, certainly in relation to the nineteenth century, 'the history of education has been written from the perspective of boys and men' (Burstyn 1977: 18). In the UK Purvis, in particular, insisted on the need to develop feminist accounts of both working-class women and middle-class women in the nineteenth century. She argued that the history of women in nineteenth-century Britain should be approached in terms of a 'domestic ideology' that located women within the home as full-time wives and mothers. The ideals of femininity that were involved in the domestic ideology were class-specific, so that the image of the middle-class 'perfect wife and mother' was separate from that of the working-class 'good woman', and led to different kinds of struggle over access to education and the form and content that such education should take (Purvis 1983). Purvis and others explored the detailed implications of this approach in a number of works during the 1980s (Burstyn 1980; Dyhouse 1981; Purvis 1989b).

Nevertheless, there remained a strong view among such authors that the field as a whole was stubbornly resistant to the direct challenge posed by feminist theory. For example, when Flett (1989: 145) asserted that 'the capitalist system was, and is, all about inequality and division, but at root the issue was more of class than sex', Purvis protested, in reply, that 'the overriding concern with social class has obscured the role of women in history and the inequalities that women, in comparison with men, experienced because of their sex' (Purvis 1989a: 148). The male-centred accounts that were characteristic of historical research in the British context, she continued, had led to an emphasis on men as the makers of educational history, a focus on education as being mainly for boys and men, and the trivialization of the experiences of girls and women. Overall, she contended, 'British history of education seems remarkably slow to respond to the challenges that feminist history poses. While feminist researchers document and chart the history of women's education, their findings remain ghettoised and isolated from what is seen as the "main body" of work' (Purvis 1992: 263–4). On the other hand, some of the familiar problems of the uncritical application of theory were also evident in this area of research, and a new generation of historians of women has begun to challenge the findings of this earlier feminist sociological history. For example, Theobald (1996) suggests that the idea of 'double conformity', coined to help to describe a process of strict adherence on the part of educators and educated to both standards of ladylike behaviour and those of the dominant male values and structures that were in operation, is itself suspect. According to Theobald, the notion of double conformity is 'present-centred' in a way that 'locks the historian into a perception of failure in the past', a perception that may not have been felt by contemporaries. Furthermore, she argues, 'The notion of double conformity is also overly dependent upon prescription, that is, upon what was supposed to happen rather than what did happen' (Theobald 1996: 212; see also, for example, Bourke 1998; Weiler and Middleton 1999; Nolan 2000).

Developing from this new interest in gender relations has been the emergence of research examining masculinities (for example, Lingard and Douglas 1999), and this has also begun to inform historical research in the area of education (Tosh 1999 is a recent discussion with interesting implications for education). Ideals of 'manliness', it has been suggested, can be understood from many different intellectual perspectives, including sociology, literary criticism and religious studies (Mangan and Walvin 1987: 2). Victorian patriarchal values, in both Britain and the United States, have been investigated in detail. For example, Springhall has examined attempts to build 'character' in British boys through the extension of Christian manliness to working-class adolescents, as seen in the Boys' Brigade and in juvenile literature (Springhall 1987). Research on the role of sport in education has also emphasized its significance as a means of constructing masculine and feminine distinctions in society (Mangan 1986).

Sociological concern with the effects of changing educational policies on the relations between the classes and the genders has been especially marked in research on the history of school teachers developed, for example, by Lawn, Ozga and Grace in Britain and Apple in the United States. This work has sought to document the social class relations of teaching that underlie teachers' 'professionalism', the inequalities faced by women teachers and the recent ways in which the state has encroached increasingly on teachers' work. Grace (1978: 1–2), for example, has argued that teachers in state schools constitute 'within any type of social formation, a crucial sector of the agents of cultural and social reproduction and a *crucial sector of the agents of symbolic control*'. Teachers of the urban working class, he continues, 'can be seen historically *to have been* the objects of class control and supervision but this emphasis has overshadowed study of the ways in which some of them resisted the system of which they were a part and sought to turn it to other ends' (p. 2). Attempts to locate the teachers of the urban working class as a 'strategic occupational group', therefore, need to involve 'some examination of their historical origins and formation and some examination of their position as the nexus of continuing ideological conflict within state education' (p. 3). From these propositions Grace then embarked on a historical discussion that sought to trace such developments over time and to understand their outcomes in the present day. Similarly, Apple, a leading American sociologist, has also attempted to develop a historical account of teachers informed by social theory, emphasizing that

> By focusing only on the current situation, on the current attempts to restructure curriculum and teaching, we lose a sense of what these attempts grew out of. Very importantly, we can also miss some of the major political dynamics that are embodied within such attempts. In so doing, the efficacy of real groups of people who successfully acted against such earlier periods of rationalisation is lost.
>
> (Apple 1986: 10)

More recent sociological work of this nature includes Lawn and Grace (1987), Ozga (1988), Hargreaves (1994) and Lawn (1996). During the 1990s, such work tended to suggest a sharp break from the practices and structures associated with a historical period of 'modernity', in some cases (for example, Hargreaves 1994) leading to an exploration of the likely implications of 'changing times' or 'postmodernity'. Some historians have taken issue with aspects of this sociological history of teachers and their work, and are highly sceptical of the rather vague historical understandings embodied in such literature. For example, McCulloch *et al.* (2000) challenge the idea of a complete 'break with the past', and point out that underlying continuities as well as discontinuities can be found in the position of teachers over the period from the 1940s to the 1990s. Meanwhile, from within the tradition of historical sociology, Green (1994) has strongly criticized postmodern accounts of state education and is dubious about the global shift in education policy and practice which they claim to identify. Nevertheless, this literature as a whole constitutes a significant and continuing contribution to a historical understanding of school teachers, and recently has helped to provide the basis for theoretically informed histories of teachers and teaching, such as Rousmaniere (1997) and Rousmaniere *et al.* (1999).

Although much sociological analysis of education systems and curricula has remained insular, some international and comparative work in the sociology of education has been attempted from a historical perspective. Proponents of this approach have argued that, in the absence of comparative dimension, historical sociology of education lacks a key gauge for judging the nature and extent of change in a particular national context. At the same time, the sociological dimension is seen as crucial in providing the basis for generating the theory and overarching models with which to compare national patterns of development in education.

Archer's (1979) major enquiry into the social origins of education systems makes a strong case for using both historical and comparative evidence in order to gain an understanding of how education systems develop and change. She argues that the distinctive role of sociologists is to generate theoretical understandings: 'If sociology is to add to the work of the educational historian and the comparative educationalist it must be by developing theories which over-arch their findings' (p. 1). She describes her work as a 'macro-sociology of education', which involves 'the examination of two things and the relations between them':

> On the one hand, complex kinds of social interaction whose result is the emergence of particular forms of education: on the other, complex types of social and educational structures which shape the context in which interaction and change occur. The sociological task is thus to conceptualise and theorise about the relationship between these two elements. Its aim is therefore to provide an explanation of how social interaction produced specific kinds of education in different countries and how, from within this context, further interaction succeeded in introducing change.
>
> (Archer 1979: 4)

Archer's approach to this problem is based on a Weberian analysis, which she suggests allows her to give equal emphasis both to the limitations that social structures impose on interaction among individuals and to the opportunity for innovation, or 'agency', that the instability of such structures tends to present. She seeks on this basis to provide a theoretical framework that will account for the major characteristics of national systems of education, and the main changes that such systems have gone through. Overall, she comments, her approach seeks 'to capture those factors which historically have moulded education in different countries, and to develop a set of propositions which explain these national patterns' (p. 42). In extending her general macrosociological theory to these macroscopic educational problems, she uses the educational systems of England, Denmark, France and Russia as her frame of reference.

Other studies have been developed with a similarly broad purpose. Ringer's *Education and Society in Modern Europe*, also published in 1979, focuses on what it calls the 'comparative social history' of national systems of secondary and higher education (p. 1). He emphasizes the need for a historical approach in order to explore the 'inertia' of educational systems, or the 'consequence of accustomed expectations'; in his view, such an approach 'distinguishes the underlying reality of an educational system from the unstable surface visible in ordinary political narratives or in accounts of individual institutions'. Like Archer, he is insistent on the importance of the comparative approach to education systems as a means of achieving adequate explanatory power as to how and why each has developed in a particular way:

> There is simply no other means of arriving at explanations, and not just descriptions, of change in education. One must be able to separate characteristics unique to this or that national system from traits shared by several systems. This sort of discrimination, in which the generality of causes is related to the generality of their effects, is an indispensable step in the construction of adequate explanations.
>
> (Ringer 1979: 1)

In Ringer's study, state education systems are seen as partly autonomous rather than simply as adjuncts to other social processes or institutions, and he emphasizes that in different historical phases they have retained a great deal of independence from the economy. He develops a detailed comparison of the German and French systems of education, and then suggests further comparisons with the UK and US systems. His analysis of the social effects of education systems is developed further in a subsequent study of structural change and social reproduction in the rise of modern educational systems in Germany, France and the UK between 1870 and 1920 (Muller *et al.* 1987). Other contributors to this later work, in the spirit of Ringer's study, focus on the social effects rather than the economic contexts of these education systems: 'The educational systems that emerged from the structural changes of that crucial period, it seems to us, ended by perpetuating and reinforcing the hierarchic organisation of their societies, and we really want to ask just how this came about' (Ringer 1987: 3).

Similarly, Andy Green's account of the formation of national education systems in nineteenth-century Europe and North America develops an explicitly sociological approach. According to Green (1989: vii), 'exactly why modern systems of education arose, and why they arose at different times and in distinctly different forms is a challenging problem and one which has been surprisingly neglected within historical sociology.' He investigates the education systems that were established in the UK, France, Prussia and the United States in order to determine the social factors that underlay their development and to analyse 'specific national differences in the chronology and forms of the development of public schooling' (p. ix). His analysis focuses on the role of the state in promoting education systems in different countries, and concludes that the formation of national systems 'occurred first and fastest in countries where the process of state formation was most intensive' (p. 310). The nature of class relations in society was also important in determining the purposes of schooling in the different societies studied: 'It was the different forms of hegemony operating between the dominant and subordinate classes which was ultimately responsible for what schools did, for who they allowed to go to what kind of school and for what they taught them when they were there' (p. 311). In the UK case, the relative weakness of the state was decisive in ensuring that the education system was developed later than in the other cases studied and with an emphasis on diversity and independence, in such a way that it was 'last to create a national education system', and 'never quite completed the job' (p. 316; see also Green 1997).

Comparative sociological study of the nature of school curricula has also been initiated; for example, in the work of Meyer *et al.* (1992), which investigates world models and variations among national patterns for the primary school curriculum. This focus on curricula as well as systems is an important development in such comparative analysis, and could well be developed further. The tensions between national identity and the forces working towards globalization – centrifugal and centripetal in nature – will also no doubt attract increasing attention from historical sociologists. Recent collections on the themes of 'national identity' and 'globalization' which evoke these tensions may be found in *History of Education* (1999, vol. 28, no. 3), and *Journal of Education Policy* (1999, vol. 14, no. 1), respectively.

The enlarging vision

It is clear, then, that the working methods and interests of sociology have had a major impact on historical research in education, and that this influence is continuing to develop. In addition, especially over the past two decades, a wide range of other social sciences – psychology, economics, geography, anthropology – have also made a significant contribution to the field, and have done so when undertaken both as a distinct endeavour based on a specific discipline and as part of interdisciplinary research. In the process, such analyses have posed a challenge to the traditional methods of historical research in education.

Psychology has often been seen by historians of education as a negative force, partly because of its predominant emphasis upon individuals rather than the broader social context they inhabit, but also because of its role during the twentieth century in helping to rationalize and promote educational inequalities through such devices as the intelligence test. Critical treatments of the role of psychology in the history of education, indeed, have constituted a significant literature for the writing of which some understanding of psychological theory is required. Brian Simon, for example, embarked on a master of education course at the University of Manchester in the late 1940s in order to help to inform his critical study of mental testing, and recalls in his autobiography that this helped him to formulate a challenge to 'the hegemony of mental testing which legitimated the highly selective system now emerging up and down the country' (Simon 1998: 59). More recent critical studies, such as that by Evans and Waites (1981), have similarly attempted to draw on psychological theory in order to fashion historical analysis of 'how this psychology has functioned as an ideology and as an instrument of social administration and selection' (p. x).

By way of contrast, in the 1980s and 1990s new contributions have been made to the historical literature on mental testing that have been either 'neutral' in tone (Sutherland 1984) or avowedly sympathetic to the role of educational psychologists and psychological theory in the rise of a 'meritocracy' in England and Wales (Wooldridge 1995). Like Simon, Wooldridge suggests that 'The history of educational psychology points to the intimate links between psychological theory and more general issues of policy and politics.' (p. 14). However, his interpretation of these historical links is very different from that of Simon and other critics:

> For the psychologists who dominated educational thinking for much of this century were meritocrats rather than conservatives and progressives rather than traditionalists. They combined a passion for measurement with a commitment to child-centred education. Their work was inspired by a desire to open admission to established institutions to able children, regardless of their social origins, and to base education on the natural process of child development. They found their most articulate supporters on the left and their most stubborn opponents on the right. In theory, their arguments were subversive of the social hierarchy; and in practice they provided important opportunities for able working-class children to rise into the elite.
>
> (Wooldridge 1995: 16–17)

Such debates among historians are informed, in part, by sociology and politics and by continuing controversies over selection devices in education, but they are also dependent on an understanding of psychological theory and practices. Historical writing on child-centred and progressive education has demanded such expertise. Walkerdine's research, for example, explores the implications of Piagetian psychology in relation to early years education (Walkerdine 1984), while Brehony details the character and effects of the Froebel movement in late nineteenth-century England (Brehony 1998).

Latterly, too, psychology has begun to be deployed in the sense of applying theories drawn from psychology in order to understand historical issues in a fresh way. Its obvious potential for the study of educational biography has been acknowledged (Kridel 1998). Its relevance to pedagogy, such as the emotional characteristics and 'maternal' notion of teaching that has often developed, especially in primary schools, has also been addressed. As Steedman (1985: 122) has pointed out,

The outline of an educational history that can be called the feminisation of a trade, can be turned right around, and we can see that in classrooms, as in the middle-class nurseries of the nineteenth century, the understood and prescribed psychological dimensions of modern good mothering have been forged – and forged by waged women, by working women – by nurses, nannies and primary school teachers.

Other areas are as yet less well developed. For instance, the nature of 'memory', including the relationship between individual and social memories, has attracted keen attention among social historians over the past decade (see, for example, McCulloch *et al.* 2000, especially Chapter 4) but has yet to be fully explored by historians of education.

The discipline of economics has also been brought to bear on historical research in the area of education. As the work of Anderson and Bowman (1976) and Lundgreen (1976) shows, there has been an ongoing debate over the relationship between educational change and economic growth that has required for its adjudication economic expertise, often of a highly specialized nature. Aldcroft (1998) documents the development of this debate in relation to the experience of rich and poor nations.

In the case of Britain, the relationship between education and economic performance has had particular relevance because of its implications for the so-called 'British disease'. Education has often been held primarily responsible for the relative decline of British industry and the economy since the nineteenth century, and economic historians have played an important role in assessing the debate in this context. Aldcroft (1992) and Sanderson (1994, 1999), for example, are highly critical of Britain's failure to develop technical schools and its emphasis on academic and liberal education for the elite. Barnett (a military historian) charts the rise of what he calls 'education for industrial decline' (1986: Chapter 11). Over the past decade, however, some dissenting and revisionist cases have begun to be advanced. Rubinstein (1993: 24), for example, argues that Britain was not fundamentally an industrial and manufacturing economy, but was rather 'a commercial, financial, and service-based economy whose comparative advantage always lay with commerce and finance'. He seeks to reassess the character of education in England and Wales in the light of this view, and concludes that there was no 'haemorrhage of talent' from the key areas of commerce and finance by those with elite schooling that would provide an explanation for long-term trends in the British economy (Chapter 3). Meanwhile, in a parallel study Pollard (1989) tackles the evidence for maintaining that German scientific education and technical education was ahead of that in Britain by 1914. He demonstrates not only that government investment was equivalent but also concludes that British schools and training programmes matched the demand of British employers for skilled personnel, findings which serve to switch the focus of discussion from the appropriateness of the curriculum to the competitiveness of British firms. In similar vein, Szreter (1997) suggests that it is sustained national commitment to investment in all the nation's human resources that constitutes the key to maintaining high rates of economic performance over the long term in a competitive international market. He therefore seeks to widen the historical debate from its established focus on the provision of scientific education and technical training, to embrace the provision of human resources in a wider sense that includes the social services alongside health and educational institutions. 'By contrast with the British experience', he suggests, 'the world's long-term economic high performers, notably the Germans and Japanese, have more consistently and more generally invested in the promotion of their nation's total pool of human resources through a wide range of institutions' (p. 101).

The debate over the 'British disease' also serves to highlight the increasingly interdisciplinary nature of social scientific contributions to historical research in this area. Wiener's (1981) study of English culture and the decline of the industrial spirit raised important yet elusive issues about the relationship between cultural values and attitudes, and economic and industrial decline. According to Wiener, a 'cultural *cordon sanitaire*' or 'mental quarantine' encircled the forces of economic development such as technology, industry and commerce (p. ix), and he found in the 'shaping of a gentleman' through the English independent schools perhaps the prime exemplar of his general case. More broadly, too, other recent research has begun to shed light on the social, political and ideological dimensions of issues that have usually been presented as 'economic' in nature. In the United States, the curriculum historian Herbert Kliebard (1990) has suggested that policy initiatives in technical education have been less important for their economic instrumentalism than for their role as a form of 'symbolic action' that involves a potent 'use of language to organise allegiances, perceptions, and attitudes'. Vinovskis (1995: Chapter 5), also in the United States, explores the views of Horace Mann of Massachusetts on the economic productivity of education to demonstrate the political character of his arguments. The imagery of economics and its effects on educational provision have also begun to be investigated. For instance, Reese's (1998: 255) research shows in an American context how 'values about work, capitalism, the character of American democracy and the nature of humankind informed not only courses in political economy, history and government, but in particular the wider range of school subjects comprising the course of study'. The social effects of the application of 'markets' as a principle in educational provision have also begun to be studied in depth (for example, Marginson 1997).

Geography provides a further major example of the application of the social sciences to the history of education. In the British context, the research of W. E. Marsden has been especially significant for its detailed exploration of the historical geography of education. As Marsden (1987) himself suggests, his academic training, which included a first degree in geography and a higher degree in educational history, provided him with 'the impulse and hopefully also the capacity to work comfortably in the disciplinary borderlands' (p. xiv). He makes a convincing case for including 'spatial factors' as a framework in the history of education, on the grounds that, as he contends, 'Educational phenomena are distributed in space, and by definition enter the sphere of interest of the geographer' (pp. 5–6). Marsden's work explores problems of scale (national, regional and local), social distance, sphere of influence (for example, catchment areas) and diffusion (spatial as distinct from temporal and social). He applies these problems to understanding educational inequalities in nineteenth-century England, leading him to conclude that 'Social stratification, territorial segregation and educational graduation comprised an interactive trinity, implicated in enabling the English school system to reproduce inequality' (Marsden 1992: 125).

Many of the issues raised through this set of perspectives are exhibited most vividly in the urban arena. As a result, research on the history of urban education has also emphasized geographical dimensions (see, for example, Reeder 1979; Goodenow and Ravitch 1983; Goodenow and Marsden 1992). Ecological theory in urban sociology is also applied to the history of education in this context. The nature of housing, transport and other social services is seen by such authors as integral to an understanding of educational provision in this kind of milieu. In general, Marsden insists, these applications demand an interdisciplinary perspective on the history of education, although he is careful to endorse not 'the eldorado of some grand, all-embracing explanatory synthesis', but instead 'the more limited notion of mutually beneficial partnership' (Marsden 1987: 16). Finkelstein perhaps has something more ambitious in mind when she calls for historians of urban education 'to go beyond the study of structure, beyond the analysis of macro-politics and economics, beyond the study of the work of elite planners, to include the study of experience, of small face-to-face social contexts and processes, the consciousness of reformers and the educational experience of ordinary people' (Finkelstein 1992a: 174). She continues:

> To bring these dimensions of urban educational experience into view, historians of education will need to conceptualise cities as cultural and psychological as well as material and intellectual environments. They will need to analyse the work of educational elites in psycho-social as well as structural terms. They will have to view education as something experienced as well as planned – a process of interaction between learners and teachers.
>
> (Finkelstein 1992a: 174)

The study of urban educational history also suggests incorporating and applying recent scholarship on childhood (for example, Sutherland and

Barman 1992), youth (for example, Springhall 1986; Hendrick 1990) and popular culture and the media (for example, Springhall 1998).

Anthropology is no less promising, although as yet it is less well developed in relation to the study of educational history. Nevertheless, pioneering studies exist which have opened up important fields of study. In Britain the husband and wife team Iona and Peter Opie built on their groundbreaking study of the history of nursery rhymes (1951) with a classic study (1959) of the traditional lore and language of school children based on teacher observation in 71 schools which they then related to a mass of printed sources from the sixteenth century onwards. They followed this in 1969 with a similar study of children's street and playground games. In France in 1960 Philippe Ariès effectively opened up single-handedly modern scholarship of childhood in history with his work *Centuries of Childhood* (English translation 1962). In the process, its wide-ranging exploration of values and symbols – *mentalities* – helped to fashion an emerging sub-discipline of historical anthropology. More recently, Thomas has contributed penetrating essays on school discipline (1976), literacy (1986) and numeracy (1987) in pre-industrial England, all informed by ideas from modern social anthropology yet scrupulously grounded in sixteenth- and seventeenth-century sources. Also in this vein is the interesting study by Hobsbawm and Ranger (1983) on 'tradition', which, as they point out, is invented at particular points in time for social and political reasons. In nineteenth-century England, as they show, the 'invention of tradition' was a means of establishing or reinforcing the status of particular social institutions, and of defining the ways in which they were to develop. Independent ('public') schools and universities were notable in taking advantage of this method of sustaining their own authority, which in turn defined the role of other institutions in relation to them. McCulloch (1988) applies this analysis to the case of Auckland Grammar School in New Zealand. Current research is also beginning to explore the implications of ethnohistory, especially as a means of understanding the history of native or indigenous education, or describing the cultural past (Marker 1999). So far, however, as Marker (2000) contends, 'The sharing of disciplinary approaches between anthropology and history has been a prominent methodology in research about Indian–white relations in North America, but for the most part, ethnohistorians have not been interested in schooling as a topic for inquiry.' It would appear that the same holds true elsewhere in the world. As with the other disciplinary perspectives that have been discussed in this chapter, it seems likely that such pointers will expand significantly in the years ahead the scope of historical enquiry in education.

As we have noted at several points, however, the application of 'theory' derived from the social sciences carries with it perils no less than possibilities for the unwary researcher. Case study 2, focusing on the ways in which the highly influential ideas of the French intellectual Michel Foucault have been used to inform historical study, serves to highlight a range of problems with which historical researchers in the field of education need to engage.

Case study 2: Foucauldian interpretations

Over the past twenty years, many historical researchers have set out to use the insights of Michel Foucault to help to explain and interpret the nature of historical change in education. These efforts have been based principally on readings of Foucault's work *Discipline and Punish: the Birth of the Prison*, which was first published in French in 1975 and translated into an English edition two years later. Foucault argued that the character of punishment underwent a fundamental transformation during the eighteenth century, from the public spectacle of executions to a system of 'constraints and privations, obligations and prohibitions' (Foucault 1977: 11). As a result, according to Foucault, 'a whole army of technicians took over from the executioner, the immediate anatomist of pain: warders, doctors, chaplains, psychiatrists, psychologists, educationalists'. In Part II of the study, he explored some of the ways in which newer forms of discipline produced 'docile bodies'. Among these, he emphasized the role of elementary education; for example, through the development of the modern classroom.

> In the eighteenth century, 'rank' begins to define the great form of distribution of individuals in the educational order: rows or ranks of pupils in the class, corridors, courtyards; rank attributed to each pupil at the end of each task and each examination; the rank he obtains from week to week, month to month, year to year; an alignment of age groups, one after another; a succession of subjects taught and questions treated, according to an order of increasing difficulty.
>
> (Foucault 1977: 146–7)

This 'organisation of a serial space', in Foucault's view, made possible 'the supervision of each individual and the simultaneous work of all' (p. 147). The educational space began to function as a 'learning machine', but also as 'a machine for supervising, hierarchizing, rewarding'. The instruments of this new disciplinary power were what Foucault described as hierarchical observation, normalizing judgement and the examination. Hierarchical observation, or the 'disciplinary gaze', was based on techniques that involved continual surveillance. Normalizing judgement defined values and standards that established both homogeneity and individuality. The examination combined both of these techniques to create 'a normalising gaze, a surveillance that makes it possible to qualify, to classify and to punish' (p. 184).

Foucault's precepts have been widely accepted as a means of understanding the character of modernity, and therefore also of addressing the changing conditions of the late twentieth century, which in the view of many sociologists constitute the onset of 'postmodernity' (see, for example, Usher and Edwards 1994, especially Chapters 4 and 5, and our discussion in Chapter 3). Many historians of education have found Foucault's ideas especially suggestive. As has recently been noted, his writings 'have informed the work of many historians of education who are rethinking the discourses, practices, and effects of modern compulsory state schooling' (Rousmaniere *et al.* 1997: 7). They have done so by offering new ways of looking at 'the discursive and disciplinary pedagogical practices through which we are differently constituted as subjects, and through which we come to know ourselves as unique individuals' (p. 8). This has often involved asking new questions of existing historical sources, as, for example, Curtis sought to do in his Foucauldian history of public elementary schooling in west Canada from the late 1830s to 1871 (Curtis 1989, 1992). However, such interpretations of educational history have also raised basic difficulties and proved in several instances highly controversial.

First, Foucault's general model is often at odds with the detailed findings of historical researchers. For example, his emphasis on the rise of the classroom in the eighteenth century sits uncomfortably with the research of historians such as Hamilton (1989) and Reid (1990) who have located it in the sixteenth and early seventeenth centuries. Hoskin has usefully discussed this problem of the reliability of Foucault's historical model. One of the earliest historians of education to explore the implications of Foucault's analysis, Hoskin demonstrated the value of Foucault's interpretation of examinations in helping to explain the 'rational authority' of modern schooling. As Hoskin (1979: 146) suggested, Foucault had launched 'a new investigation of the links between knowledge and power at the largely unconscious level where the parameters of the thinkable are set', and in so doing had formed a new agenda or broad project for historical researchers to investigate and explore (see also Hoskin 1982). On further reflection, however, Hoskin also pointed out that Foucault 'got his history of the examination wrong' (Hoskin 1990: 45), particularly by seeing it as an eighteenth-century invention rather than deriving from the emergence of the European university in the twelfth century. But this more critical understanding of the limitations and problems of Foucault's historical model does not lead Hoskin to dismiss his contribution. On the contrary, it generates a new appreciation of the development of examinations: 'The point that I would stress about Foucault is that despite the egregious errors in his history, he had that ability, or knack, or nose even, for sensing the significant. Now it is our task – humbler but still important – to broaden and deepen the furrows he ploughed' (Hoskin 1990: 48). Hoskin suggests that this involves a re-reading of earlier historians such as Ariès (1960) to try to resolve and develop their interpretations of this topic, somewhat like the approach taken in our case study on the school curriculum and classroom in Chapter 1.

Among historians of education Selleck (1991) has also warned against uncritical application of Foucauldian concepts and terminology. He suggests that they often tend to mystify and confuse issues rather than to illuminate them. According to Selleck, the terms that are repeatedly employed in such accounts, or 'Foucault-speak', 'do mystify, do make the obvious seem challenging, do help the reader to think that questions are answers, do accord privilege to theory which is checked against little, except perhaps another unchecked theory' (p. 92). Once 'lost in this mire', he complains, 'obvious questions slip away'. Nevertheless, Selleck also accepts that 'exciting and challenging' insights can be generated through Foucauldian devices. Overall, then, Foucault's work may be taken to demonstrate the value of social theory for suggesting avenues of enquiry in historical research, the problems of its uncritical application and the importance of a critical engagement between hypotheses and empirical study.

A further issue is that of how to take account of different historical and national contexts in applying a Foucauldian analysis. It can be highly problematic to apply a set of principles that derive from a specific location and time, and import them into a different historical and cultural context. Kirk and Twigg (1994), for example, use Foucault's *Discipline and Punish* in an attempt to provide an underpinning theoretical framework for their research on eugenics, anthropometrics and school medical inspection in Victoria, Australia, in the early twentieth century. Employing characteristically dense terminology of the kind criticized by Selleck, they set out their aims:

> The terms regulation and normalisation of the body are adapted from Foucault's work and are used consistently throughout this paper to refer to the ways in which the broad range of human movements, from simple to complex, are channelled and contained within time and space through subtle processes of learning, training and imitation . . . The containment and organisation of human bodies needs to be seen, following Foucault, as a complex process of 'docility-utility', of simultaneously constraining and enabling, rather than as an oppressive regime of coercive control. Consequently, the practices which constitute corporeal regulation are part of the fabric of everyday life and comprise a mosaic of what Foucault terms 'little practices'. It is the argument of this

paper that school anthropometry and medical inspection are two sets of such practices.

(Kirk and Twigg 1994: 35)

They acknowledge criticisms that Foucault's approach is problematic when applied to Australia – for example, because of the relatively small working-class population until after the Second World War – and concede that 'Foucault's analysis of French society cannot be applied simplistically to Australia' (p. 35). Nevertheless, they insist, 'the concepts generated in Foucault's work concerning the mechanisms and processes of corporeal regulation and normalisation (rather than "social control"), properly contextualised, are informative means of theorising the processes of *schooling* in its broadest sense, especially where this process was aimed specifically at children's bodies' (pp. 35–6). It is the phrase 'properly contextualised' that goes to the heart of the matter here. That is, determining proper contextualization is a key task of the historical researcher in applying social theory or models to a specific time and place.

Conclusions

In this chapter we have not attempted to be exhaustive in mapping the emerging contribution of the different social sciences to the historical study of education. Other examples could have been added to those we have given and other research fields on the cusp of contributing to our understanding of the educational past could have been discussed: linguists and critical theory, health research and disability studies, organization theory and management, information studies, communications, computing and media studies. Moreover, such a comprehensive survey is hardly within our scope, given that much of this research has, as we have emphasized, been interdisciplinary in nature and thus tangential to the mainstream historical methods about which this book is concerned.

Overall, an enlarging vision may be seen in the contribution of the social sciences to historical studies in education, and especially since the 1980s. Sociological insights and theories have been pre-eminent since the 1940s, and reached the apogee of their influence on and penetration into the field in the 1960s and 1970s. Since that time, sociology has continued to be a potent force and remains undoubtedly the most influential of the social sciences in this regard, but it has increasingly been joined by other social sciences which have provided, separately and together, significant and interesting insights and new lines of research. This broadening range of social scientific influences has far from run its course, and is perhaps the most likely source for reappraising the way in which historical research in educational settings is seen and will be undertaken in the future. These influences greatly enrich the study of educational history. Yet, at the same time, they raise difficult problems of historical interpretation and contextualization, the tackling of which involves critical and sceptical engagement with theory rather than its straightforward and unquestioning application.

Furthermore, just as historical researchers must engage with theory, they also need to adopt a critical relationship with the sources at their disposal. This remains the bedrock of historical method and it is to practical issues of the types of historical sources and evidence available in the field of education that we turn in the next two chapters. However, these issues are not entirely divorced from the theoretical and historiographical debates that we have so far outlined. Far from it, in fact, for as we will see in Chapter 7, the intentions of the researcher help to determine the nature of the sources that are examined and how they are interpreted.

5 | Using published sources

It has been suggested that 'The study of the history of education is blighted by a proliferation of "histories" resting precariously on reminiscence and anecdote, loose generalisation and crude, functionalist assumptions' (Slee 1986: 3). If this is true, then it is especially important for researchers specializing in the field to develop a clear notion of what source materials are available for study, how to gain access to them, the choices involved in using them and the problems that relate to their deployment. As in other areas of historical research, an important distinction is generally drawn between *secondary* and *primary* sources. Of the latter, the key types are various kinds of *documentary* records and *oral* evidence. Each of these kinds of source has particular uses and limitations, and we explore these with particular reference to the problems of historical research in education. In this chapter we focus mainly on published secondary and primary sources and online sources which are relatively easily accessible to the researcher; in the following chapter we extend the discussion to the use of unpublished documentary sources and oral evidence.

Primary and secondary sources

As a general rule, there are two major differences between the primary sources and **secondary sources** used in historical research. The first is about authorship: whereas primary sources are produced by those directly involved in or witnesses to a particular historical episode or issue, secondary sources are written after the event, usually by those who were not party to it. Primary sources therefore provide the researcher with first-hand accounts; for instance, of a committee meeting or an educational practice, or of more broadly based discussions of contemporary education. These accounts will have been produced in the first instance with a particular aim and audience in view, and it is always important for the researcher to seek to understand these in order to appreciate the perspective adopted by the author and therefore the potential biases and interests involved.

Secondary sources are accounts and interpretations of historical events or longer-term processes. These are produced at some remove from the events or issues in question, and may thereby have greater detachment. However, they are influenced by the assumptions and problems of the society and context in which they are written, and often the author has a great deal of commitment to specific aspects of the study and their interpretation. In some cases, the author of a secondary source may have been involved in some way in the events or issues under discussion; for example, Simon (1991) was a prominent protagonist in the events that he is describing. It is therefore necessary for the researcher to understand the potential biases and interests of secondary sources just as much as those of primary sources.

The second key difference between primary and secondary sources, deriving from the first, concerns availability. While primary sources may take a range of forms and may be difficult to find, secondary sources are generally available in published form. However, in practice this distinction is not always as straightforward as it may appear. For example, some primary sources exist also in published form, produced in a convenient format for a contemporary audience. New technologies and formats are helping to erode these differences further as previously restricted material is being made more widely accessible, especially through the Internet. It may be necessary for the historical researcher to seek suitable primary sources in conditions of restricted access, such as archives, and this is still the most broadly characteristic requirement of such research. However, it may be possible to undertake most or even all of the relevant research needed for a study by making use of the holdings of a well provided university library.

Primary and secondary sources are therefore not rigid and distinct categories. Moreover, it is also possible for a particular source to be both primary and secondary in nature. A book on the history of public (independent) schools in England written during the Second World War, for example, may be treated as a secondary source on the history of the public schools and as a primary source on attitudes towards the public schools during the Second World War (see, for example, Mack 1941). It may be necessary for researchers to be able to read source material in both ways, depending on the kind of study that they are developing. Furthermore, where a secondary source exists in more than one edition historians should always consider carefully which edition or editions they need to consult, depending on the kind of analysis they undertake.

In the following discussion of different kinds of secondary and primary sources, then, the examples used should be regarded not as rigidly demarcated types but in terms of a continuum. At one end of this are secondary sources written at a distance from the topic being examined and generally accessible to researchers. At the other end are primary sources produced close to the event or issue being explored and difficult to access for researchers.

Using secondary sources

The most common kind of secondary sources for historical research in education are published books, articles in academic journals, chapters in edited collections and unpublished masters and doctoral theses. Such works examine specific historical problems or debates in education by interpreting primary and secondary sources on the topic. Thus, for example, Tyack and Cuban, in the United States, develop a general historical argument about attitudes to schooling during the twentieth century on the basis of a wide range of evidence in order to draw their own conclusions:

> Schools can easily shift from panacea to scapegoat. If the schools are supposed to solve social problems, and do not, then they present a ready target. In recent years, allegedly worse schools have been blamed for lack of economic competitiveness and other societal problems. Some observers have interpreted the supposed decline of education as a trumpet call to reform public schools. Others, believing that public education is beyond repair, have argued that the way to regenerate schooling is to create a market system of education in which parents can choose their children's schools, either public or private, and pay the tuition through vouchers funded by taxes.
>
> (Tyack and Cuban, 1995: 14)

In other cases, such as the following, the views of earlier scholars, or secondary sources, are discussed before the author puts forward an alternative interpretation:

> The education of English gentlemen in the first half of the seventeenth century combined several distinct traditions. Most scholars have emphasized the long-term effects of the educational boom of the sixteenth century, characterized by attendance of gentlemen at university and the widespread employ of tutors for teaching the Latin classics, which created for the first time a national culture of humanist inspiration. Yet the first half of the seventeenth century also saw foreign travel and education grow in importance, as the itineraries and ethos of what became the Grand Tour of the eighteenth century began to take definitive form.
>
> (Motley 1994: 243)

Secondary sources such as these are reliant upon existing scholarship on particular topics, and also suggest specific new perspectives or analyses by which to understand the problems involved.

There are several specialist journals in the history of education available for researchers. These include the following:

1 *History of Education:* an international journal edited from Britain (bimonthly from 2000); it is the journal of the British History of Education Society (this Society also publishes a useful *Bulletin* twice yearly which includes shorter articles as well as information about relevant conferences, archives and other resources in this field, including a series of occasional publications, guides to sources in the history of education and lists of theses completed).

2 *History of Education Quarterly:* an international journal based in the United States (quarterly), which is the journal of the United States History of Education Society.

3 *History of Education Review:* an international journal based in Australia and New Zealand (biannual); it is the journal of the Australian and New Zealand History of Education Society.

4 *Journal of Educational Administration and History:* a biannual journal based at the University of Leeds in the United Kingdom, an institution which has also generated a valuable series of scholarly monographs in the area.

5 *Historical Studies in Education:* a triannual international journal based in Canada.

6 *Paedagogica Historica:* an international journal based in continental Europe which publishes articles in several different languages (quarterly); it is the journal of the International Standing Conference in the History of Education (ISCHE).

7 *Histoire de l'Education:* a specialist journal in the field (quarterly) based in France.

8 *History of Universities:* an annual publication edited from Britain that focuses specifically on higher education in an international context.

A number of very useful works of reference are available that support detailed historical research in educational settings, and it is important to consult these at an early stage. For example, biographical dictionaries on leading educators in Britain (Aldrich and Gordon 1989) and in North America and Europe (Gordon and Aldrich 1997) contain much valuable information. A useful guide has been compiled for British government publications in education during the nineteenth century (Argles 1971), and also the twentieth century (Argles and Vaughan 1982). An edited volume with a comprehensive index of all letters relating to education that were published in *The Times* of London from 1785 until 1910 (Leinster-Mackay with Sarfarty 1994) is another very helpful research tool in this area. Such specific reference works may be used alongside more general works that include educational references, such as Cook's volumes listing the archival collections of leading public figures and organizations in nineteenth- and twentieth-century England (Cook 1994).

There is also a very wide range of secondary source materials that may be drawn upon in relation to the history of education. These include studies that were published thirty or more years ago. Among these older studies are some that have achieved 'classic' status because they have been widely used and cited by others, and have come to be regarded as key works on particular topics. Often these have different concerns and are based on different sets of assumptions than would be the case today, but they are still worth consulting, because they represent particular kinds of approach and philosophy to which we can relate our own. For example, one of the earliest of modern works on the history of education produced for an English readership, the Rev. R. H. Quick's *Essays on Educational Reformers* (first published in 1868), provides an extensive chronological treatment of the ideas of the 'great thinkers' in education from the Renaissance to the nineteenth century. Quick was frank about his own predispositions and preferences, as in the case of the German educational philosopher Friedrich Froebel: 'All the best tendencies of modern thought on education seem to me to culminate in what was said and done by Friedrich Froebel, and I have little doubt that he has shown the right road for further advance' (Quick 1895 edn: 384). His hopes for the development of a 'science of education' through an understanding of educational reformers may seem unconvincing a century and more later. Even so, his work still constitutes a helpful starting point for research on this topic.

Foster Watson's major study *The Beginnings of the Teaching of Modern Subjects in England*, published in 1909, is another classic work that seeks to explain the 'general movements' that led to the inclusion of modern subjects in English education, attempting to set out 'the historical facts with regard to the beginnings of the teaching of modern subjects in England . . . in connexion with the history of the social forces which brought them into the educational curriculum' (1971 edn: viii). It was the first work that attempted to do so in a single volume in the English context, and it succeeded in providing a thorough yet accessible treatment of the topic that continues to command close attention. Indeed, it was reprinted as late as 1971 on the grounds that 'it still remains the basic source work and has yet to be superseded' (p. v). Ivor Goodson, emphasizing the importance of studying the history of the curriculum, has even more recently acknowledged and tried to build upon the work of Foster Watson (for example, 1988: 49–50).

General studies of the history of education are also useful starting points for research, especially for their frameworks of analysis, the kinds of sources that they make use of and the way they treat particular topics. In the British case, for example, there is a range of such works published since 1945 on which to build. Curtis's book on the history of education in Great Britain (1948) traces educational issues from the medieval period. Barnard's work (1947), originally entitled *A Short History of English Education from 1760 to 1944*, attempts what it describes as a 'bare outline' of developments over this time (1961 edn: v). Armytage (1964) surveyed 400 years of English education from the 1560s. Lawson and Silver (1973) collaborated to provide a 'social history' of education since its Anglo-Saxon beginnings. Simon's four-volume work on the history of English education since 1780, which took over thirty years to complete (1960, 1965, 1974, 1991) is also very useful as a point of reference.

Making use of such published sources is important not only for new researchers in the area, but also for more experienced authors who are seeking a fresh approach to familiar themes. Thus, for example, Stephens (1999), explaining how he has set out his discussion of education in Britain from 1750 to 1914, emphasizes that he wants to avoid what he sees as the 'arid and unhistorical' approach of much earlier writing on the history of education, which, he claims, 'used to be concerned with "Acts and Facts" recorded almost in a vacuum and divorced from the general history of the period in which they were set' (p. x). Nor does he wish to dwell unduly on the role of education in national politics, or on the development of institutions and administrative structures, because he feels that there are already enough studies of such topics. Rather, he concludes, 'I have preferred to limit detailed treatment of political and administrative matters (though not to ignore them) and to give more space to aspects of the relationship between education, society and the economy which have concerned social and economic historians in recent years' (p. x). It is his reading of earlier secondary sources that has helped Stephens to define his own approach to the subject.

When approaching more narrow or specific topics in the history of education, too, an understanding of the contribution of earlier studies is a vital prerequisite. On secondary education in England in the nineteenth century, for example, there is again a wealth of secondary sources available, from Archer's classic study (1921), through the two-volume work of the American historian Edward C. Mack on the development of the 'public' (that is, private) schools (1938, 1941), to Roach's more recent research (1971, 1986, 1991). Similarly, approaches to research into the history of women's education in the nineteenth century require a foundation in the work of recent scholars who have often differed significantly from each other in their predispositions, sources and conclusions, such as Bryant (1979), Burstyn (1980), Purvis (1989b) and Martin (1999); or, in relation to longer-term frameworks in the history of women's education, Kamm (1965) and Purvis (1991). Research into the history of childhood will also benefit greatly from study of Philippe Aries's *Centuries of Childhood*, first published in 1960, even though its central arguments have been fiercely contested and largely superseded over the past forty years.

While we emphasize the importance of such well established and influential works as a basis for new research, it should also be noted that many other contributions, much more obscure and less often cited, can be useful for the same purpose; for example, histories of schools by former pupils or teachers. Works on specific institutions or on highly specialized subjects may pass unnoticed by contemporaries, but raise issues that seem more important to later generations. For example, J. H. Simpson's pamphlet on the public schools and athleticism, published in 1923, attracted little attention at the time except in striking, as J. A. Mangan (1986: 1) comments, an 'unpleasantly discordant note amid applause which had begun some sixty years earlier and which, in an atmosphere of post-war nostalgia, had risen to a crescendo'. Simpson's study formed a useful point of departure for Mangan's important work on the topic sixty years later, Mangan (1986: 1) contending that 'This book, therefore, is an attempt to rectify a longstanding omission.' Moreover, as well as making use of these older secondary sources, it is necessary to make a thorough study of recent and contemporary publications; such material often comprises a huge range of research that has to be carefully assessed as a preliminary to trying to build on and reorient existing knowledge and understandings. One important class of such literature, often overlooked, is that of masters and doctoral theses. Most are substantial studies in their own right, most are as rigorously researched as the best published studies and often they draw on source material and methods that may differ from those encountered elsewhere.

A literature review of this kind is a basic feature of any study in any academic field. In a historical study, however, it seems worthy of special emphasis for several reasons. First, history itself involves understanding roots and influences often over long periods, and it is appropriate for historians to demonstrate their commitment to this breadth of scope in their reading of secondary sources. Second, historians are able to apply particular skills to this task; for example, in showing how previous work on a topic has developed in relation to broader educational, social, political and other changes. Moreover, historians are especially well equipped to essay a *critical*, contextually informed review of previous studies in terms of their strengths and limitations in helping to develop the focus for new research in the area. Finally, it is necessary to conduct such an exercise when undertaking historical research in education because this field has produced a particularly large amount of published work over the past century that requires critical evaluation.

Published primary documentary sources

Primary documentary evidence of various kinds has been the single most important source for historical research in education. As in other areas of historical research, appropriate documents, or written texts, are not always easy to locate, and require careful assessment and interpretation (Scott 1990 is a useful general work on the use of documentary sources in social research; see also Platt 1981). Many documentary sources that might have provided valuable evidence about the development of education have not survived, either because of accidental loss or through deliberate disposal of records, which has unfortunately been a widespread practice in many educational institutions. Of those that remain available for researchers, some provide extensive documentation of particular themes and topics, while others are scanty and give only partial clues.

As far as education over the past two centuries is concerned, common types of primary documentary source include policy reports, committee papers, correspondence, autobiographies, diaries, school log books, school and university magazines and textbooks, newspapers, photographs, cartoons and caricatures, local registers and works of fiction. This wide array of potential sources may be grouped first in terms of ease of access. Some primary sources may be found in online or published form, and are readily available for study through a networked computer or in most libraries of higher education institutions. Others are unpublished, and may only be found in private hands or in restricted conditions of access in archive collections. In the remainder of the present chapter, we concentrate on documentary sources that are published or easily accessible to researchers.

Online primary sources

Primary sources that are accessible online through the Internet and websites constitute the fastest growing and potentially one of the most significant forms of primary source material available to researchers (see Crook 1998). This is a new and rapidly changing area in which websites are being continually created and changed, and information about them quickly becomes out of date (see also Smeaton 1999 for detailed information). The kinds of websites that need to be consulted for British studies include:

1 Library catalogues and bibliographic and archive sources. For example:
  http://opac97.bl.uk (British Library)
  http://www.hmc.gov.uk (Historical Manuscripts Commission)
  http://www.education.bids.ac.uk (British Education Index)
  http://www.ihrinfo.ac.uk (Historical research for university degrees in the United Kingdom: theses completed)
2 Academic society and journal home pages. For example:
  http://ihr.sas.ac.uk/ihr/education/hoes.html (History of Education Society, Great Britain)
  http://www.tandf.co.uk/jnls/hed.htm (History of Education)
  http://ihr.sas.ac.uk/ihr/education/ische1.html (International Standing Conference for the History of Education)
3 Administrative and governmental sources. For example:
  http://www.open.gov.uk/dfee/dfeehome.htm (Department for Education and Employment, Britain)
  http://www.parliament.the-stationery-office.co.uk/pa/cm/cmhansrd.htm (*Hansard*, proceedings of the Houses of Parliament in Britain)

http://www.nfer.ac.uk (National Foundation for Educational Research)
http://www.scre.ac.uk (Scottish Council for Research in Education)
http://www.bera.ac.uk (British Educational Research Association)

There are also many other online sources that may be valuable, including bookshop catalogues, university teaching resources, newspapers, datasets and primary e-texts (for a general discussion of history and the Internet, see Gorst and Brivati 1997).

Printed primary sources

Examples of primary sources published in print include the following.

Specially edited collections

These consist of selections of material collected into convenient book or other accessible form for ease of reference. They are often a valuable source for students, especially when the full and original materials are not accessible. Generally, however, they provide only preliminary clues for historical research, partly because they usually do not include the full work, and partly because the editor of the collection has asserted his or her own priorities in the process of selection. Gaining access to the original documents is usually the only way to overcome such obstacles, and this is always preferable where possible.

A good example of a collection of this kind is J. Stuart Maclure's *Educational Documents*, first published in 1965 and subsequently revised and updated in several editions. This brought together 'selected extracts' from leading official documents in order to plot the development of a public system of education in England and Wales since 1816. As the editor notes, it does not include 'the recondite and the recherche', but seeks to 'arrange the famous and the obvious passages in a useful form' (1968 edn: 1), and it achieves this very successfully (see also Sylvester 1970 on educational documents from AD 800 to 1816). Harold Silver's collection *Equal Opportunity in Education* (1973) pursues the same objective in relation to a more bounded topic and shorter time period (from the 1920s to the 1960s). Cohen (1974) is an attempt to document the history of education in the United States in a fuller and more exhaustive fashion (over five volumes), but is less easy to follow and digest.

Another useful source of selected material, in microfiche form, is the *Journal of Sources in Educational History*, published three times per year since 1978 with extensive extracts from official reports, papers, books and treatises relating to major issues in education. John Burnett's collection of autobiographies of childhood, education and family in Britain from the 1820s to the 1920s, *Destiny Obscure* (1982), is also a very helpful and convenient source of this type. This work provides a range of autobiographical material, originally written as part of memoirs, by working men and women during the nineteenth and twentieth centuries (see also Abbs 1974).

Published policy reports and parliamentary debates
Policy reports on educational problems and proposed developments are an important and widely used primary source for historical research. In many cases they are available for study in well resourced libraries of higher education institutions. Some policy reports are not only extensive and revealing in their own right, but also include lengthy appendices containing statistical evidence and the evidence given by individuals and organizations. The Bryce Report on secondary education (1895), the Robbins Report on higher education (1963) and the Dearing Report on 16 to 19 year olds (1996) are major British examples of this kind of quarry of information and contemporary opinion. Others, while shorter, provide valuable statements of influential approaches to and perspectives on education, such as the Norwood Report on the curriculum and examinations in secondary schools (1943) and the 1992 report *Choice and Diversity* (Department for Education 1992). Parliamentary debates on educational issues, recorded in *Hansard*, are another valuable source of information and discussion relating to the United Kingdom.

Contemporary books and treatises on education
A vast number of books and general treatises have been written over many centuries that address the educational issues of their day, and these comprise fertile source material for historians. For the modern era in England, these include such works as H. B. Smith's *The Nation's Schools* (1927), which may be compared with other contemporary works such as Cyril Norwood's *The English Tradition of Education* (1929). Similarly, the views expressed by J. H. Newsom in *The Education of Girls* (1948) may usefully be compared with those of Kathleen Ollerenshaw's *Education for Girls* (1961) as a convenient means of approaching attitudes towards the nature and purposes of education for girls in post-war England. The collected published works of specific educators, such as the early twentieth-century Chief Inspector Edmond Holmes (Gordon 1983), can often comprise a significant corpus of historical material for analysis.

Autobiographies
Autobiographies are another easily accessible primary source for historians, albeit that they depict educational issues and events looking back often after many years or even several decades. This can have an important distorting effect in that some details can be forgotten or misplaced, and the nature or importance of the events being recalled tends to be adjusted to suit the writer's overall view of their own life (see Swindells 1995). There are again many instances of published autobiographies that have significance as

potential sources for historical research in this area. Examples include F. H. Spencer's *An Inspector's Testament* (1938), which reviews his early struggles as a pupil-teacher in England in the 1880s, going on to examine his later role in administration, which culminated in a position as Chief Inspector under the London Education Committee. Lord Eustace Percy's *Some Memories* (1958) is another helpful and widely used British source, in this case with material on the writer's work as President of the Board of Education in the 1920s and on the changing educational scene. Politicians' memoirs such as this proliferated in the 1980s and 1990s to form a wide range of often conflicting sources on the development of education and the problems of educational policy in the later decades of the twentieth century (British examples include Callaghan 1987; Baker 1993; Thatcher 1995).

David Vincent's (1982) study of nineteenth-century working-class auto-biography is based on 142 autobiographies (published and unpublished), which he describes as a 'rich vein of source material' that had received surprisingly little 'serious attention' among English historians (p. 3). He acknowledges that this neglect is at least in part 'a product of unresolved doubts about the "truth" and "relevance" of works which are necessarily subjective in form and limited in number' (p. 4). All sources are subjective, he continues, but the subjectivity of autobiography encapsulates rather than merely qualifies its meaning, in the sense that it constitutes not a 'collection of remembered facts', as with other sources, but 'a pattern of recollected experiences' (p. 5). According to Vincent, this presents a distinctive kind of opportunity for historical researchers: 'More than any other form of source material, autobiography has the potential to tell us not merely what hap-pened but the impact of an event or situation upon an actor in the past' (p. 6). Moreover, it is a source that is of particular relevance to education, since nearly all the autobiographies involved in Vincent's study devote a sec-tion to accounts by authors of their education, 'no matter how transient and superficial it might have been' (p. 94). As Vincent concludes, 'If their con-cern often seems out of all proportion to the meagre schooling they received, we are presented with sufficient information to form a picture of both the consumer's experience of elementary schooling in this period, and the sig-nificance which working men attached to the subject' (p. 94). These auto-biographies are also centrally concerned with education in a different sense, involving, Vincent suggests, diverse attempts by the authors 'to use the materials and skills of written communication to come to terms with their situation . . . [and] the forces which controlled their lives' (p. 109).

Newspapers and periodicals
The press is another major published source for educational historians. During the twentieth century, especially, a specialized educational press developed that provides an invaluable running commentary on events and developments. In Britain, this includes *The Times Educational Supplement*,

established in 1910 (see, for example, Simon 1989 on the role of the *TES* during the Second World War), and *The Times Higher Educational Supplement*. Other educational periodicals which proved to be less durable but that are key sources for their own period include *Teachers' World* and the *Journal of Education*. Other, more general, newspapers and periodicals can also be key sources for education. For example, the *Manchester Guardian* from the 1920s through to the 1940s offered informed and critical insights on the major educational issues of the time, especially through its editorials on education which were contributed by the leading educational reformer R. H. Tawney (McCulloch 1996). The cartoons in the humorous periodical *Punch* offered irreverent views about educational issues (Smith 1998). For the period since the Second World War, and especially since the 1970s, the growing diversification of the media provides a wide range of potential sources for historians in this area, including, for example, television broadcasts (Crook 1999).

Cunningham (1992) examines the image of the teacher as portrayed by the British press over the period 1950–90. In order to achieve this, he compares newspaper coverage at twenty-year intervals, in 1950, 1970 and 1990, in the unofficial 'newspaper of record', *The Times*, and in the leading mass circulation 'tabloid' newspapers of the political left and right. From this evidence, he discerns a decline in the professional status of teachers over the period, but also 'distinct continuities' in the representation of teachers as professionals (p. 55), and some indications of the beginnings of a renewed benign perception of their role.

Works of fiction
Novels, short stories, children's books, comics and other works of fiction can also constitute important published primary documentary sources. Often such works have provided dramatized or entertaining versions of reality that convey profound truths about education or particular educational settings. Thomas Hughes's *Tom Brown's Schooldays* (1857) has been widely used as a source on independent ('public') schools in England in the nineteenth century (for example, Honey 1977). *Roaring Boys*, by Edward Blishen (1955), is a fictionalized account of 'Stonehill Street', drawn from Blishen's own experience as an English teacher in a secondary modern school in London (see also Spolton 1962; McCulloch 1998: esp. 87–90). Other works have considered the significance of, for example, school stories since the nineteenth century (Quigly 1982), children's fiction in Jacksonian America (MacLeod 1975, 1976) and British university fiction since the 1940s (Carter 1990).

School textbooks
Very often textbooks will reveal a great deal about the curriculum and often about pedagogy or teaching styles, although it is important not to assume

that what is included in a textbook is always what is taught or learned. They reflect the aims and purposes and the underlying assumptions of the educational process, often in vivid ways. The crude racial stereotypes of the school textbooks of early twentieth-century England (Marsden 1990) are an important example of this, as are the patriotic and xenophobic tendencies of the British and American textbooks studied by Grosvenor (1999) and Foster (1999). Such school textbooks often went through many editions and can be found in libraries as well as in second-hand book shops.

Using published primary sources

In developing a full understanding of the nature and potential use of published primary sources, it is important to clarify the following key issues:

1 Issues relating to the *text*. Scott (1990) approaches the study of documents by asking four key questions about the text: (a) its 'authenticity' or genuineness – 'whether it actually is what it purports to be' (p. 19), as far as its contents, authorship and date are concerned; (b) its credibility – that is, how sincere and accurate it is as a record; (c) its representativeness – how representative it is of documents on a particular topic, including those that have not survived to the present day or are otherwise unavailable for research; (d) its meaning – to 'decipher the script and translate the language into the linguistic forms current in the community of researchers of which the investigator is a part' (p. 28). This involves close textual analysis of the source to understand its argument and its general nature as an account, and the extent to which it is internally consistent. A short piece illustrating the 'textuality' of an article in the *Times Educational Supplement* in December 1917 is Campbell (1999), which points out that 'all experience is filtered by the participants (including the researcher) and is subject to context, pretext, subtext, intertext and intratext' (p. 18). Codd (1988) is a fuller discussion of the analysis of educational policy documents with the purpose of penetrating the ideology that they embody, and of exposing what he calls 'the real conflicts of interest within the social world which they claim to represent' (p. 30). Pursuing these goals also entails exploring the following areas.
2 Issues relating to the *author*: who produced the work, in what circumstances, for what purpose; how it relates to their other work before and afterwards; what is known of their life and career and of their associations that may help to explain the nature of this source.
3 Issues relating to the *context*: what were the circumstances in which it was produced? This includes the immediate context surrounding the production of the work – for example, its role as a contribution to a continuing public debate on an educational problem – and its broader

context, including the educational changes taking place when it was published, the nature of social and cultural changes at this time, local and
national political issues, economic developments and international or
global changes.

4 Issues relating to the *audience* of the work: who was it intended for? A
limited audience based on locality, or social class, or gender, or ability to
pay, or other restricted group? Or was it intended to be accessible to a
broad audience without obvious restrictions?

5 Issues relating to the *influence* of the work: did it achieve the results that
it intended? This is an especially interesting and difficult issue in relation
to education, where practices in schools and other educational settings
have often differed from public admonition and policy.

6 The *processes* involved in its production: origins, development and consequences. Often these can be visualized in general terms through the
construction of a time-frame that includes both the chronology of events
that were directly relevant and contemporary developments in education,
politics and society. However, access to published sources alone will
usually make it difficult to ascertain the detailed processes at work in pro-
ducing such documents.

7 The *interests* that underlay its development and the interactions that it
involved between different groups and individuals. Again, it is not always
easy to discern such interests from published records except in clear cases
of open and public disputes.

These issues may be illuminated most clearly through reference to specific
examples. Case study 3, on the concept of the 'Alternative Road' developed
by the Crowther Report of 1959, briefly examines each of these in turn with
reference to the use of published sources.

Case study 3: The 'Alternative Road'

McCulloch (1989) examines the history of the secondary technical
schools which were developed in England and Wales from the 1940s
until the 1960s. They were intended to provide a different kind of education from that of the academic grammar schools, but were largely
unsuccessful, being abandoned in the 1960s when comprehensive
schools for all abilities and aptitudes became widespread. The govern-
ment-sponsored Crowther Report, *15 to 18* (Ministry of Education
1959), supported the aims of the secondary technical schools and
argued in favour of their further development.

Text: Chapter 35 of the Crowther Report outlined a 'practical
approach' in education that would appeal to pupils who were not
attracted to or motivated by 'the academic tradition which inspires

and is embodied in our grammar schools and universities' (p. 391). It suggested that there were 'two kinds of minds', which should be approached in different ways (p. 394). The first kind of mind was the academic type, 'which is readily attuned to abstract thinking and can comprehend the meaning of a generalisation' (p. 394). On the other hand, it continued, 'there are other minds which cannot grasp the general except by way of the particular, which cannot understand what is meant by the rule until they have observed the examples' (p. 394). In short, it asserted, 'Some minds are analytical; others can only build up' (p. 394). The latter type, which 'reason better in non-verbal ways', were 'not necessarily inferior', and more provision should be made for them. The full-time academic route might not be suitable for such pupils and might not attract them, while the part-time route was 'narrowly vocational' and not always available. The Report argued that it should be a major task of English education to 'construct a new system of education for the years between 15 or 16 and 18 which would neither suffer from these defects of the part-time route nor be academic in the old conventional sense' (p. 394). This would depend on rehabilitating the word 'practical' in educational circles, and defining it more clearly. It might be encouraged in the schools, according to this Report, by promoting secondary technical schools, some of which had already shown themselves capable of developing 'a practical education making progressively exacting intellectual demands' (p. 397). The Report acknowledged that such education was only in its 'early stages of development'. It recommended therefore that further enquiry should be made into the problems associated with the general idea of the 'alternative road'.

Author: The Crowther Report was produced by the Central Advisory Council for Education (England), which had been set up under the Education Act of 1944. In March 1956 the CAC was reconstituted and asked by the then Minister of Education, Sir David Eccles, to examine the education of boys and girls of between 15 and 18 years of age. The chairman of the CAC during this enquiry was Geoffrey Crowther, from whom the Report took its name. Crowther was Deputy Chairman of the Economist Newspaper Ltd. He was born in Leeds, educated at Leeds Grammar School and Oundle School, and then achieved a double first in economics at the University of Cambridge. His education and background were therefore such as to give him insights into both the 'academic' approach and 'practical' concerns. The Committee itself comprised 27 members, of whom seven were from the universities, two from the local education authorities, two from technical colleges, seven from schools (maintained and independent), one from the field of teacher training, two from trade unions, two from employers and three from elsewhere. Members with a particular interest in the 'practical route' included Dr H. Frazer (head of a leading secondary technical school, Gateway Boys' School in Leicester), Dr Peter Venables (Principal of the College of Advanced Technology in Birmingham) and George Bosworth (Chief Technical Personnel Administrator at the English Electric Company).

Context: The Report was intended to investigate ways of encouraging a further expansion in educational provision for boys and girls after the statutory school leaving age, which was then 15. Its proposals on the 'Alternative Road' were central to these broader goals. The educational context was one in which the secondary technical schools were struggling to survive as separate institutions, and to attract public attention. The Ministry of Education itself appeared increasingly uncertain as to their future prospects. Meanwhile, the Ministry was defending the grammar schools against criticisms that they were promoting social inequalities through such devices as the eleven-plus examination. In May 1959, the author C. P. Snow attracted widespread interest with his Rede lecture on the two cultures and the scientific revolution, which emphasized the distinctions in English education between the arts and sciences, and the narrowness of the specialization that took place in school sixth forms and universities. In terms of the political context, the Conservative Party had held power since 1951, and gained its third consecutive general election victory in October 1959. The Prime Minister, Harold Macmillan, pointed to a trend of rising affluence to suggest that most people were more prosperous than ever before, and that social class divisions were obsolete. The further expansion of education and science promised to provide additional support for the new 'welfare state', and also to maintain Britain's economic competitiveness and military capability, especially in the face of the apparent military threat of the Soviet Union. As the Crowther Report pointed out, 'today, it seems to us that education is generally thought to be a "nation-building" investment fully as much as part of the welfare state' (p. 55).

Audience: The Crowther Report was submitted to the Minister of Education, Geoffrey Lloyd, with the prime aim of influencing government policy in the area. However, it was intended for a wide readership, and made clear that it had been written 'for the general public, whose rising interest in all educational matters is one of the most encouraging developments of recent years' (p. xxxi). It conceded that it included many special terms and usages in its detailed discussion of educational issues, but endeavoured to assist the general or non-expert reader by appending a glossary. It was published (priced 12s. 6d.) by the Ministry of Education on the grounds that its recommendations 'are of great importance and will need to be studied very carefully not only by the Government but also by the many other interests concerned, including parents' (p. viii).

Influence: Many of the recommendations of the Report were adopted, but the idea of the 'Alternative Road' failed to gain government support. In a debate on the Crowther Report in the House of Commons in March 1960, Sir David Eccles on behalf of the government praised it warmly, but avoided committing the government to carrying out its proposals, probably in part because of its extensive financial implications. The *Times Educational Supplement* condemned the mixture of 'vague assurances and pious hopes' offered by Eccles in the House of Commons debate, and concluded: 'The government has looked at the Crowther Report and has decided to do nothing about it . . . When the history of our present education comes to be written it will surely be seen that with chances unseized and opportunities lost Monday was its sorriest day' (*TES* 1960). No further enquiry into the development of an Alternative Road was established. Within five years, the secondary technical schools were virtually swept away when a new Labour government under Harold Wilson encouraged the spread of comprehensive schools. On the other hand, the leaders of the secondary technical schools took fresh heart from the support offered by the Crowther Report, and began to develop alternative strategies to promote an 'Alternative Road' for all secondary schools. These initiatives were developed further by the Schools Council for the Curriculum and Examinations, which was established in 1964. A Project in Technology was launched by the Council in 1967, which attempted to build on some of the ideas of the Crowther Report. Donald Porter, a Craft Inspector who was a key figure in the creation of this Project, also wrote a curriculum bulletin entitled *A School Approach to Technology* (Schools Council 1967), which acknowledged a lasting debt to the Crowther concept.

Process: The time-frame suggested for the Crowther committee and its 1959 Report (Figure 5.1) depicts some of the major educational, social and political developments that took place during its three-year period of gestation. These are suggestive in indicating significant influences on this process, but they do not allow analysis of the internal debates of the committee itself over this time. They also leave problematic an understanding of causation, or the precise relationship between these contemporaneous developments.

	Committee	Educational change	Social/political
1956	Set up	White Paper *Technical Education*	Suez crisis
1957		Hailsham Minister of Education	Macmillan Prime Minister
1958		Lloyd Minister of Education	'Affluent society'?
1959	Report published	C. P. Snow's *Two Cultures*	General election

Figure 5.1 The Crowther Report: a time-frame.

In this chapter we have suggested that it is possible to carry out a great deal of useful and detailed historical research in education through the use of published and widely accessible sources. Nevertheless, there are other cases in which it is necessary to make use of less accessible source material or of different kinds of sources, and it is to these that we turn in the next chapter.

6 | Methodological issues

In this chapter we continue our discussion of research sources by looking first at the less accessible types of primary documentary sources in relation to different educational settings, then at some uses of visual sources, and also at issues of 'quantitative' and 'qualitative' analysis of primary sources. We follow this with an examination of the uses of oral history in the field of education, before concluding with some reflections on the strengths and also the problems of a pluralist approach that seeks to combine different sources and methods in examining a particular educational issue.

Unpublished primary sources

Unpublished primary documentary sources in restricted access in public or private collections may for our purposes be divided into three general categories: those relating to educational policy and administration; those of individual educational institutions such as schools and universities; and those comprising the personal papers of teachers, educational reformers and others whose work has related specifically to education at a particular stage in their lives.

Education policy and administration

The main repositories of primary sources on education policy and administration are the public records offices. In England and Wales, for example, the most important of these is the Public Record Office, located at Kew in south-west London. Morton (1997) is a helpful guide to the education records held at the Public Record Office. These include the nineteenth-century records of the Committee of the Privy Council on Education and the Education Department, and those of the Board of Education (1899–1944), the Ministry of Education (1944–64) and the Department of Education and Science (from

1964). The records of the major commissions and reports on education are deposited here, together with files on the development of elementary and primary education, secondary education, technical and further education and universities. Office files reflect the development of official policy on many different aspects of education.

There are several important points to take into account when using public records such as these in Britain. First, the records are 'weeded' before they are classified as public records, often several times, so that only those that are regarded as being historically significant are retained for this purpose. Second, most of them fall under the 'Thirty Year Rule', which means that they cannot be accessed until at least 30 years after the event. In practice this can be significantly more, since if a file runs over several years it will only go into the public domain when its most recent item is over 30 years old. Some kinds of files, such as school inspection reports, are subject to a 50 year rule. These restrictions on access obviously place important limitations on what can be effectively researched. They do not apply in all countries, and legislation requiring freedom of information can enable researchers to gain access to particular files. In some countries, public records on education are accessible to researchers with no or very few restrictions, which makes it possible to conduct research on very recent and contemporary administrative and policy issues. For example, in New Zealand in the 1980s and 1990s changes in secondary school catchment zoning policies over the previous 30 years, and their implementation in different local districts, could be researched on the basis of the records of the Education Department, which would have been very difficult if not impossible to achieve in Britain (McCulloch 1991). Third, such files usually include the annotations of the officials and politicians involved in developing policy, so that the researcher gains some access to the thinking that underlay it, and the differences and tensions involved.

As well as the national public record offices, there are also county record offices, which are useful for the study of local administration and policy. The records of local education committees are located here, together with relevant sub-committees and local reports. These are subject to restrictions similar to those of the national record offices. Gosden (1981) points out that the preservation and accessibility of local education authority (LEA) records varies 'a good deal from place to place'. But where they are available, 'the scholar may hope to obtain from local authority records a great deal of help in studying local ways of applying education policies in such matters as school organisation, building, finance, the recruitment of and employment policies concerning teachers, further education provision, governing bodies and so forth' (p. 89; see also Sutherland 1981). Gosden and Sharp (1978) is a useful example of a detailed study of one LEA, the West Riding in Yorkshire.

Where it is possible to gain access to them, these unpublished records have major advantages over published sources for the study of education policy and administration. It is still necessary to pay due regard to the text, the author, the context, the audience and its influence, just as much as for a published source. Indeed, there are often interesting and important issues that arise from these aspects of study. For example, it may be difficult to ascertain the author of the document, and the audience is often limited to a small group designed for a particular purpose. In addition to these general aspects, however, unpublished records also allow deeper insight into the processes and interests involved. It is often possible to trace the development of a specific issue or phenomenon in much more detail with the use of unpublished sources, whether over the short term of a few years or a decade, or over the longer term embracing generations or a century or more (see Silver 1990). Moreover, political debates and contestation are often expressed much more clearly in documents designed for private circulation among only a small group or with close colleagues. In investigation of these themes with the help of unpublished source material, the time-frame developed can be much more detailed and may also incorporate the internal developments involved in the production of a document. Waring (1979) provides a helpful example of this kind of time-frame in relation to the emergence of the Nuffield Foundation Science Teaching Project, which was established in Britain in 1962 (see Figure 6.1).

In relation to the case study of the Crowther Report of 1959 elaborated at the end of Chapter 5, unpublished departmental documents shed much light on the reasons why the 'Alternative Road' failed to win immediate approval. The files of the Ministry of Education, held at the Public Record Office in London, show that ministry officials held strong objections to the ideal developed in the report. A. G. Gooch, senior HMI for technical schools, expressed strong criticism of the idea of two different 'types' of pupils that was pursued in Chapter 35, 'a concept for which, in my view, there is very little positive evidence'. He argued instead that all pupils should be encouraged to develop a wide range of abilities: 'We need to work on the assumption that every individual will develop his "ideas" and his academic studies more successfully if they are associated with realities whenever this is feasible, and when they are applied to practical situations, and looked at in relation to future applications in a chosen career.' It would therefore be wrong, he insisted, for official policy to encourage 'the concept of two different "types" of pupils rather than encouraging the association and full development of the two "types" of ability within each individual pupil' (A. G. Gooch, memorandum, 'The Alternative Road' ('15 to 18', Chapter 35), 4 March 1960; located in Ministry of Education file ED.158/29, Inspectorate papers on secondary technical education, 1956–64, at the Public Record Office, London). Meanwhile, the further education branch of the ministry raised quite different objections, suggesting that the idea of the 'Alternative Road' was simply too vague to be considered further:

	Events and organizations	Industry	SMA and AWST	The Nuffield Foundation
1949–54	Manpower forecasts	Shortage of technical staff Aids for teachers British Iron and Steel Federation course for teachers	Shortage of teachers Teaching of science in secondary modern schools Prep. school science Links with industry	'Education' added to Trust Deed, 1950
1955	de Witt's study	Industrial Fund		Grant to Royal Institution minor grants to help science education
1956	UNESCO conference on science teaching	Shell inquiry (BAAS)	UNESCO conference memorandum	
1957		Shell: Annual Conference (Industry and Science)	Science and Education Committee *Policy Statement* Panels set up	
1958	BAAS Conference on school science			
1959	First Minister for Science Snow: 'Two Cultures'	Esso Senior and Junior Loan Service		
1960	Studley Conference	Shell conference on modern methods in teaching science and maths		
1961	Professional Bodies involved	BP conference – teaching of science and maths Salters conference	Revised *Policy Statement* & Part I Syllabuses Barrow Court Conference Opening of SMA HQ SMA/AWST proposal	Dinner at Nuffield Lodge on school science Sir Alexander Todd → NF NF proposal Trustees' Meeting, 8 December 1961
1962	4 April 1962	Public Announcement of		Nuffield Foundation Science Teaching Project

Figure 6.1 Growing involvement in school science, 1945–62.
Source: Waring (1979)

Crowther has in mind in this chapter (Ch. 35) not merely the provision of more technician courses, but the provision of full-time or sandwich courses, either in schools or colleges of further education, of a practical rather than an academic kind, for an ill-defined category of people in various walks of life who are said to stand in the same relation to the fully-fledged professional as the technician does to a technologist. It is not easy to say just what kinds of people he has in mind, and since he does no more than suggest a further enquiry, it is not proposed to pursue this recommendation for the time being.

(Ministry of Education file ED.136/930: Further education branch, conspectus of action on the Crowther Report, review of recommendations, September 1960; at Public Record Office)

In this case, then, unpublished departmental records reveal much about the problems facing the Crowther Report and its recommendations that it would not have been possible to discover through the analysis of published evidence alone.

National and local organizations
National and local organizations provide another major source of primary evidence on the history of education policy and administration. Some of these organizations are specifically educational in character; for example, teacher unions and subject teaching associations. The records of such organizations can often be found either at the organization itself or at a university-based archive or special collection to which it has been donated. They are often not subject to a 30 year rule even where they include records of negotiations with public bodies or involvement in official committees, and so they can be especially illuminating on recent developments, although conditions of access do vary. Some universities have built up important collections of organizational sources relating to the history of education. In England, the University of Warwick, the Institute of Education in the University of London, and the University of Leeds are among the most notable of these, although many other collections are available for research in other locations. Useful examples of these records include the following:

1 Association of Education Committees, representing local education authorities from 1904 until its demise in 1977 – University of Leeds Special Collections.
2 Association for Science Education, representing school science teachers since its formation in 1961, and its predecessor organizations – University of Leeds Special Collections (see Layton 1984).
3 National Union of Teachers, the major teachers' union, especially for teachers in elementary and primary schools – University of Warwick Modern Records Centre.

4 Association of Teachers of Domestic Science – University of Warwick Modern Records Centre.
5 Incorporated Association of Assistant Masters – University of London Institute of Education Special Collections.

The records of non-educational organizations are often just as important, as they constitute other major interest groups which have in many cases invested a great deal of time and activity either to general involvement or to specific initiatives in education. Examples of these include:

1 Trades Union Congress – the national organization representing trade unions in Britain, with a major archive collection based at the University of Warwick Modern Records Centre (see Griggs 1983).
2 The Confederation of British Industry – the main national organization representing employers in Britain, also with its records housed at the University of Warwick Modern Records Centre.
3 Women's Local Government Society papers – London Metropolitan Archives, London.

In many cases, research on the history of educational policy and administration needs to use a combination of published and unpublished sources, and it may also be necessary to bring together a range of unpublished sources from different national and local repositories to develop a clear and detailed explanation of a particular episode or problem. For example, researchers have sought to understand the development of educational policy during the Second World War by combining published and unpublished evidence and this has often led them to very different conclusions (compare Gosden 1976; Jefferys 1984; Simon 1986; Barber 1994; McCulloch 1994).

Educational institutions

Research on specific educational institutions, such as schools, colleges and universities, and also more informal agencies of education, such as libraries, families and churches, can often be facilitated through primary documents located and stored at the institution itself. Such material is not always available, as in many cases it will have been lost or destroyed, whether this is due to the institution having moved or amalgamated, or to lack of space or unsuitable storage conditions. In some cases these primary sources have been donated to the local county records office and it is worth making enquiries there. If material has survived and is available for study at the institution, conditions of access may well vary and it is important to reach a clear arrangement on these. Useful primary sources on educational institutions include magazines, log books, pupil records and governing body and other minutes.

The magazines produced by educational institutions, often on an annual basis for their students, staff and former students, constitute an important record of the life of schools, colleges and universities. In particular, they reveal what is seen to be most important and most desirable in such institutions. Whether they confine themselves to detailed accounts of cricket scores or devote themselves to transcripts of the annual prizegiving, they tend to present an idealized and sanitized version of the institution to the outside world. An especially interesting examination of this kind of source is Mangan's (1986) study of athleticism in Victorian and Edwardian public schools, which makes extensive use of school magazines as primary sources. Mangan points out that 'the magazine in its self-appointed role is an *official* record of school life', which has therefore 'always perpetuated established values rather than challenged them' (p. 243). He traces the amount of space devoted to sport in the magazines of different public schools in England from 1866 to 1966 in order to document the rise and subsequent decline of a 'cult of athleticism'. Although often widely circulated and available in some libraries, consolidated collections of these magazines may be difficult to access except through the institution itself.

The log books or official diaries on the activities of the school completed by headteachers are also in many cases very helpful primary sources on the history of an educational institution. They vary greatly in nature from cautious records of pupil numbers and teacher movements to elaborate manifestos of the school's aims and purposes, complete with supportive press cuttings. They can often shed light on the problems of the school; for example, in the case of Wolverhampton Technical High School in the 1950s. In this instance, the headteacher's log book records the difficult negotiations with local authority officials over the completion of a new building for the school (McCulloch 1989: 142–6).

Pupil records are generally of two types: the data recorded by the educational institution on the pupil population, and the records left by pupils, students and other learners themselves. The former include class and school registers, which are very helpful for tracing such matters as attendance and progress, and in some cases for identifying links with social background through the inclusion of home addresses and parental occupations. School reports on individual pupils are also important primary sources, as are other formal records, such as punishment books. The records left by the learners are especially important for providing insights into the experience of educational processes and of the classroom situation. These include pupils' exercise books, which often demonstrate a wide difference between the official curriculum represented by the textbook and the lived curriculum encountered by the pupil.

The administrative records of the educational institution are another familiar primary source. These include the minutes of the governing body and of formal meetings of staff. Such records are often rather terse and cautiously phrased, and tend not to deal directly with issues of teaching and learning except on particular occasions; for example, when a teacher is being disciplined or a pupil expelled. School inspection reports are an important kind of source that is often held at the school as well as in the local and national records office. In some cases it is possible to find records of informal meetings of staff, relating to the curriculum or to a department, which can shed much light upon educational aims and practices within the institution. Correspondence between the principal or director of the institution and members of staff or parents and members of the public is another type of primary source material that can yield much valuable research data.

Historical case studies of educational institutions often make extensive use of a range of institutional records. Labaree's (1988) work, for example, is a detailed historical examination of the Central High School in Philadelphia from its foundation in 1838 until 1939. He points out (p. 2) that 'Fortunately, the school was aware of its own historical importance and therefore kept an extraordinarily comprehensive array of records.' He uses for his study the annual reports by the principal, faculty meeting minutes, individual records of the origins and attainment of every student who attended the school and three published histories of the school. Heward's work on Ellesmere College in England between 1929 and 1950 is mainly built around the institution's archive of 180 files of correspondence from parents to the Headmaster of the school. As Heward (1988: 16) suggests, 'These letters yield evidence about the meanings which parents, sons and the school gave to the processes whereby boys were brought up, socialised and made into men.'

The use of such records involves ethical considerations which it is most important for the researcher to observe at all times. Before starting an examination of any set of records, the researcher needs a clear understanding in the form of a written agreement of the terms on which the research is being conducted. For example, the institution involved may wish to be shown the uses to which its material is being put before it is included in a thesis or published work. In such instances, any quotes drawn from the records should be noted and sent to the institution. However, in the interests of preserving independence, the researcher will generally not wish to be tied to an agreement that allows the institution to veto analysis or conclusions drawn from the use of the records. Especially where the records identify people who are still alive, it is important for the researcher to be sensitive about their possible use, maintaining anonymity in cases where identification may cause embarrassment or offence for either personal or professional reasons.

Case study 4: The university history curriculum in the nineteenth century

Some of the issues involved in studies of educational institutions may be further illuminated through a detailed case study of a specific topic, the development of the history curriculum in English universities in the nineteenth century. Slee (1986) points out in relation to the study of the university history curriculum in the nineteenth century that 'the bulk and range of material available for consultation are enormous', and that this material remains 'largely untapped and unsorted' (p. 3). He adopts a case study method to analyse the 'dynamics of academic practice' through detailed exploration of the emergence and development of history in the universities of Oxford, Cambridge and Manchester. In examining the growth of the Oxford School of Modern History, for example, he bases part of his analysis on the papers of the college tutor C. W. Boase, one of the first teachers of modern history in Oxford, located in the library of Exeter College. These give important clues to the nature of Boase's teaching. For example, Slee (1986: 109–10) notes:

> One page of Boase's course on 'Early Constitutional History' bears minor marks of revision dated 21 October 1880, 26 April 1882, 18 October 1883, 22 October 1885, 20 January 1887. There are few factual alterations and only two instances of extra detail being appended to the text. He delivered the same lecture over a period of seven years.

At the same time, Boase's papers also include some significant clues to the learning of his students, especially through what Slee calls a 'chance survival' which provides a 'unique opportunity' to discover 'how closely one student followed his tutor's advice in composing essay answers to examination questions' (p. 111). Slee continues:

> Among the leaves of one of C. W. Boase's many notebooks an examination script has lain buried for over a hundred years. Why he kept a script which he ought to have destroyed is a matter of conjecture. It is possible that the candidate was one of his own students. We do not know, because the name has been torn out. The candidate was by no means best of his year. His paper was assessed as a high Second, not a First Class standard.

Slee surmises that Boase retained this script for reference because he and his colleagues needed to set standards of achievement in a new discipline: 'The script may have been used to set levels of attainment.' The 'chance survival' of this nameless student's paper in a college archive permits an extended discussion of the calibre of learning and the devices necessary for examination success.

Soffer's (1994) study of the history curriculum in English universities from 1870 to 1930 also makes extensive use of institutional records. She points out (p. 3) that 'A wide reading of manuscript and printed materials, not consulted before, allows me to show how the writing and teaching of history actually shaped the ethos of graduates who guided domestic and imperial government, secondary and higher education, the professions, religion, letters, and even business and industry.' She continues:

> Some records, surprisingly complete, provide detailed accounts of what people thought and did in response to identifiable provocations and events. I have also found less complete documents, relatively mute in themselves, and have combined them with other fragments to resurrect a continuing dialogue that clarifies both constant and fluctuating patterns of behaviour. University and faculty papers, the minutes and memoranda issued by tutors, professors, faculties, governing bodies, colleges, and students contribute a wealth of virgin material. Boards of faculties kept minutes of meetings; records of examination questions; written examiner's reports; correspondence about grading, standards, curriculum, teaching, and examinations; and minutes of discussions about the awarding of degrees to particular candidates. Any one set of university chronicles, such as a faculty's minutes, tend to hide more than they display. Together, these various accounts retrieve the impelling forces that affected universities and their students.

Soffer (p. 5) also demonstrates the importance of the records left by the students themselves, both as individuals and in groups:

> Without the reports of student history clubs, other remaining evidence such as examination papers implies that the subject was decided entirely by what could be readily tested in the final examinations. But student society records deny this conclusion by demonstrating a breadth and depth of interest, on the part of teachers and students, that went far beyond examination requirements.

In addition, individual student papers and lecture materials, 'which I was fortunate enough to discover' (p. 5), provide in Soffer's view a useful basis for understanding the character of teaching and learning.

Personal papers and records

The records left by particular individuals, whether prominent or obscure, can also be of major significance for historical researchers. These vary greatly in terms of the amount of material that has survived and the conditions of access for the researcher. It is especially important to observe ethical considerations about access and use in cases where the owner of the records may be unaware of their potential significance. In some cases the individual may have retained all or nearly all of the material built up over a lifetime and donated it to their former university or another institution for researchers to study. In others, what little remains may have been left in a box in an attic until a chance discovery is made or a surviving relative dies. Such papers and records are clearly of potential importance for the study of the lives and careers of teachers and other educators. They are also useful in many cases for an understanding of the contribution of education policy makers. Many collections are based in university libraries, and where anything is known of surviving family members it can be fruitful to approach them to ascertain whether any related records exist. Examples of these kinds of records in the British context include:

1 Emily Davies papers (Girton College, Cambridge).
2 R. A. (Lord) Butler papers (Trinity College, Cambridge).
3 Edward (Lord) Boyle papers (University of Leeds Special Collections).
4 Anthony Crosland papers (British Library of Political and Economic Science, London).

Educational biography, pursued with the aim of identifying the role of the individual's personal and family background in explaining their contribution to education, has been revived as a fashionable area of study over the past few years. Some interesting research has been conducted in relation to prominent policy makers and administrators, such as James Kay-Shuttleworth (Selleck 1994) and Dr C. E. Beeby (Alcorn 1999); similarly, the lives and careers of individual teachers, especially women, have been explored. In many cases primary documentary evidence from personal collections of papers has been fundamental to such research, often supplemented by personnel and other records held by the institutions and bureaucracies where the subjects have worked.

Personal collections can contain a wealth of evidence not only about the role of the individual concerned but about their wider relationships and the contexts in which they worked. One fascinating example of this is the archive of Jane Johnson (1706–59), the wife of a Buckinghamshire vicar. She left a small collection of objects, her handmade nursery library, in a shoebox that was discovered in a cupboard in the United States in 1986. As Mary Hilton (1997: 1) remarks,

The contents of this box soon became a spark that lit a veritable bonfire of academic interest and speculation as historians, literary scholars, collectors, archivists, anthropologists and educationalists discovered overlapping and complementary fields of enquiry about the nature of childhood within British cultural life over three centuries; the debates that have surrounded the texts written and read to children; the multifarious ways childish consciousness has been considered, shaped and schooled; the emotional and moral investment that has been placed in children by adults; and, most centrally, the hitherto neglected role of woman educators in early childhood.

According to Shirley Brice Heath, the fragile and tiny hand-made materials in this collection, including alphabet cards, hand-made books and lesson cards, 'suggest certain long-running patterns and values and literacy for children of families with upwardly mobile aspirations much like the Johnsons' (Heath 1997: 20). They may be compared with the commercial materials made for children during the early eighteenth century. It is also possible to relate them to the values expressed in contemporary works such as John Locke's *Some Thoughts Concerning Education* (1693), and what is usually considered the first children's book, John Newbery's *A Little Pretty Pocket-Book* (1744) (Hilton *et al.* 1997).

Returning once more to the case of the Crowther Report of 1959, which has already been discussed in some detail above, a small personal collection of one of the members of the committee is also highly valuable as a means of furnishing insights into the production of the report. Sidney Raybould, professor of education and director of extramural studies at the University of Leeds, was a member of the Crowther Committee whose personal and professional effects were left to the Museum of the History of Education at the University of Leeds. These included the minutes of the Crowther Committee, annotated by Raybould, memoranda between committee members and submissions of evidence to the committee. The minutes reflect the 'tripartite' assumptions of the committee, particularly in the way that it was immediately divided into three 'fact-finding' groups: Group A on the problems of sixth-form pupils, Group C on the less able pupils in secondary modern schools, and Group B, which 'offered the greatest difficulty of demarcation, and in certain fields might require a negative definition i.e. boys and girls not clearly falling into A or C' (CAC for Education (England), 86th meeting, 23–4 April 1956, minute 15; located in Raybould papers). The memoranda also reveal the problems that were involved in identifying a clear rationale and route for 'Group B'. The assessor of the Committee, David Ayerst, suggested that a 'unifying theme' for this area of study was still missing. He noted that the idea of 'a technical age and mechanically-interested boys and girls' had been 'prominent in all our discussions', but that it failed to provide a precise basis for a curriculum (David Ayerst, issues paper, 'Unsolved problems in Part 3' [no date], in Raybould papers). It was

. Crowther himself who suggested a possible solution to this problem. He proposed that the committee should formulate an explicitly educational rather than a mainly economic or industrial rationale for this area, so that

> the whole of this area should be gradually transformed from being primarily designed to meet industry's needs (with some education thrown in) to being primarily designed to continue the education of a large slice of the nation's boys and girls (without destroying the usefulness to industry of the present system).
> (Geoffrey Crowther, 'Note on Mr Ayerst's paper by the Chairman' (addendum to above paper), in Raybould papers)

This revised emphasis was vividly reflected in the final report, and was central to the construction of the 'Alternative Road' (see also McCulloch 1989: esp. Chapter 7).

Visual sources

Another kind of documentary evidence is **visual sources**, which have attracted growing attention from social and historical researchers over the past decade (see Prosser 1998). Long deployed as supporting evidence to illustrate themes and arguments, they can often form the basis for historical analysis in their own right (Unwin 1983 is a helpful discussion of visual sources and the history of education). They vary both in ease of researcher access and in distance from the event or problem being studied, and may be used in different cases to support research into policy, institutions or individuals. Examples of visual sources that have been deployed in relation to education are:

1 *Paintings*. Dekker (1996) examines seventeenth-century Dutch genre painting for the 'educational messages' that they transmit. In this particular cultural context, as he and other historians have shown, paintings were highly significant for their educational messages, 'presenting the image of the desired adult personality and explaining the purpose of upbringing' (p. 160).
2 *Plans*. Seaborne (1971) and Seaborne and Lowe (1977) have produced a comprehensive history of the architecture and organization of schools in England from 1370 to 1970, a work that has been supplemented by Maclure's volume (1984) on the character of school building from 1945 to 1973. These works demonstrate the key role played by school architects such as E. R. Robson of the London School Board in the late nineteenth century, who helped to develop a distinctive style for school buildings that also reflected the civic pride of late nineteenth-century English cities. Reid (1990) also shows how changing features of architecture

such as school galleries and the shift from 'schoolrooms' to segregated and age-related 'classrooms' reflected social changes and influenced education and the school curriculum.

3 *Photographs*. Unwin (1983: 36) suggests that photographs are probably the most widely available visual sources for historians of education. Even where they are artificially posed, as in school photographs of class groups or of sports teams, they can tell a great deal about hierarchies and institutionally approved images (see, for useful examples, Humphries 1981; Mangan 1986).

4 *Cartoons*. Unwin (1983) notes that of those sources that have not so far been fully exploited by historians of education, 'it is in the field of cartoons and caricature that the most exciting prospects appear' (p. 46). Political cartoons such as those carried in the humorous periodical *Punch* in the nineteenth century by John Tenniel and others often reveal much about public attitudes to changes in education (Smith 1998). Changing images of teachers are also documented in cartoons in newspapers and journals, as exemplified by Warburton and Saunders (1996).

5 *Television and the cinema*. New forms of media developed in the twentieth century, especially cinema and television, have generated important visual evidence about education. Crook (1999) provides details of programmes on British television that have been specifically devoted to issues in the history of education, and there are many others that provide interesting source material through dramatic (for example, *Grange Hill*), humorous (for instance, *Please Sir!*) or documentary (for example, *World in Action*) treatment of education. The British cinema has been no less fertile as a potential source of visual evidence, from *Goodbye, Mr Chips!* in the late 1930s, through *Blackboard Jungle* in the post-war period, to *Educating Rita* and many other examples of the genre in the 1980s and 1990s. Cohen (1997) discusses the social effects of a range of popular media in the United States in the 1950s. Archives of these kinds of sources are accessible through online databases (for example, for the British Broadcasting Corporation) and media libraries.

Alongside such visual sources, it is important also to recognize the potential role of physical artefacts of education, such as school desks and buildings, remnants of earlier periods that in many cases have survived into our own, often protected under the aegis of museums of education and of childhood (see, for example, Betts 1981 on school desks in the nineteenth century). Moreover, the records of oral media such as the radio are also of great potential value; for instance, Cox (1996) examines school music broadcasts and the BBC, 1924–47, based on records held at the BBC Written Archives Centre in Caversham and at the National Sound Archive in London.

In the remainder of this chapter we develop further this discussion of the different kinds of unpublished, archival and visual sources through some consideration of their uses as 'quantitative' and 'qualitative' source material, and also through an examination of their strengths and limitations in relation to oral evidence.

Use of quantitative source material

Quantitative methods making use of datasets such as large-scale surveys and questionnaires have attracted many historical researchers with an interest in education. Carl Kaestle, a leading American educational historian, noted that such research has been stimulated by statistical analysis, the wider availability of computer programs and the broad sociological implications of the outcomes of schooling. On the other hand, the techniques involved are unfamiliar and difficult for many researchers, and are also time consuming and expensive compared with library-based or even archival research of a qualitative nature. Nevertheless, Kaestle (1988: 67) was confident in the late 1980s that some impressive work was beginning to emerge, 'work which helps to locate the history of American education more solidly in the context of social structure and economic development'. He was also hopeful that the wider deployment of such techniques would help to sustain a 'methodological self-consciousness' among researchers in this field, which would in turn enable them to 'explore new questions, discard old assumptions, try new techniques, and attempt to meet more rigorous standards of evidence and argument'.

An early and influential advocate of quantitative history in Britain was Laslett (1965, 3rd edn 1983) whose Cambridge Group for the History of Population and Social Structure pioneered the systematic study of archival sources over several centuries to compute, among other things, literacy rates. Lawrence Stone, another leading social historian, was strongly attracted to the use of quantitative methods as a means of addressing the history of education. In the 1960s, Stone produced two seminal articles on the 'educational revolution' in England, 1560–1640 (Stone 1964), and on literacy and education in England between 1640 and 1900 (Stone 1969). Nevertheless, he remained convinced that the history of education was at a 'primitive stage', both in the collection of data and in formulating concepts, so that it was impossible in his view 'to provide more than tentative and provisional answers to the many problems involved' (1969: 69). His proposed solution to this problem was to promote the use of quantitative research in this area. In introducing a collection of articles that sought to explore the historical relationship between schooling and society, he emphasized that the contributors had tried to answer the questions involved through the use of statistical evidence wherever possible and relevant. Only where such methods were not suitable did they employ what Stone described as 'the traditional technique of a close examination of literary sources' (1976: xvii).

For example, Lundgreen (1976) made use of time-series data on school enrolment, public expenditure on education and the growth of economic output in nineteenth-century Germany to analyse possible correlations between educational expansion and economic growth. He emphasized that 'correlations do not establish cause-and-effect relationships, nor do they quantify precisely the contribution of education to growth' (p. 20), but concluded on the basis of a detailed study that for nineteenth-century Germany the rate of growth of economic output, impressive as it was, did not appear to be directly attributable to the growth of education. In the same collection, Harrigan (1976) used a wide-ranging questionnaire survey of secondary schools taken by the Ministry of Education in France in the 1864–65 school year, located in the National Archives, to explore relationships between secondary education and social structure and mobility in France in the 1860s.

In another highly instructive case, Coleman (1972) charted the incidence of education in different districts and among different social categories in mid-nineteenth-century England using evidence drawn from the official enquiries of the period and from census returns. The enumerators' books for the census returns of 1851 and 1861, available in the Public Record Office, were also examined to provide data about smaller and more clearly defined localities, and to allow links to be drawn between the incidence of schooling and the wider social structure. In developing an analysis from these sources, Coleman (1972: 406) points out that such researchers need to be clear about what kinds of issues they wish to investigate:

> The extent of the information which one takes from the books and the size of the sample must be determined by the nature of the questions one wishes to answer. Among the variables to which the incidence of schooling could be related and for which the books contain the requisite information are the ages of children, the occupations and the birthplaces of parents, the size of the family (or at least such of it as resided in the household on census night) and the child's order in the family. The size of the sample (for the numbers will usually be too great for a complete listing of households) must depend not only on the population of the chosen district, but also on which of the variables, singly or in combination, one wishes to consider, remembering that the more variables taken in conjunction the larger the sample must be to remain representative.

Coleman illustrates these points through the results of a sample taken from the 1851 enumerators' books for the first registration district of Bethnal Green in London.

Other historians of education, however, have cautioned against too great a dependence on quantitative data, including both those studies which use statistics already present in the historical record and those in which historians generate statistics from other evidence. One such sceptic is Marsden (1979). Although drawing extensively on census enumerators' returns from the nineteenth century to support his study of local school provision, he makes the point that 'quantitatively processed aggregate assessments of social situations' can effectively divorce the researcher from 'the true feel of the experience of urban life and education in the nineteenth century' (p. 31). He proposes instead an 'eclectic and pluralist' approach that values all available methodologies for what they have to offer. Thus, on this view, the aggregate data from the returns of census enumerators should be used to complement more personal materials, such as school log books, newspaper accounts, diaries and oral evidence. A more extended study by Marsden, in which he complains that educational historians have written 'so much about the aggregates and so little about idiosyncratic groups and individual reactions to educational provision' (1987: xv), serves to reinforce this judgement.

An example involving partnership between historians and statisticians is Kerckhoff *et al.* (1996), which examines the spread of comprehensive schools in England and Wales from the 1940s to the 1970s. This work examines ten case studies of the process of comprehensive reorganization in ten different local authority areas, using detailed qualitative methods based on documentary sources. The researchers were unable to make use of public records for this purpose because of the 30 year rule, but in conducting the local case studies they were able to draw on local authority records, interviews and correspondence with former administrators, some personal and institutional records, and newspapers. The study then goes on to complement these case studies with the use of longitudinal data drawn from the National Child Development Study, to which a series of multinomial logistic regression analyses are applied to help to explain the nature of local variations within the general process of reorganization.

A detailed case study on literacy in nineteenth-century England (Case study 5) may also help to illustrate the uses that can be made of quantitative data, and also some of their limitations, and the continued need for complementary types of evidence.

Oral sources

As has already been noted, although documentary sources and methods are very important tools for historical researchers, they do have limitations. Many documents do not survive, are incomplete or are not accessible to researchers. Oral history based on interviews – for example, with former teachers and students, designed for them to recall their own experiences as historical evidence – has become increasingly popular over the past decade. Spaull (1988) made several useful points about the pioneering stage during

Case study 5: Literacy in nineteenth-century England

Since Stone's (1969) highly influential article on literacy, historical attention to this theme has grown massively, and this has raised important issues in historical method. Kaestle emphasized a distinction between two different types of approach: the first concern, reflected in Stone's work, is with the 'historical sociology of literacy rates' (Kaestle 1990: 487); the second strand has attempted to analyse the uses that have been made of literacy by reconstructing who read which texts (see also Kaestle *et al.* 1991: esp. Chapters 1 and 2). Detailed research on the growth of literacy in nineteenth-century England has vividly reflected both trends.

Several historians have sought to understand patterns of literacy in nineteenth-century England through recourse to quantitative evidence derived from sources that show the extent of the ability of adults to sign their names. These include, in particular, marriage registers. From the Marriage Act of 1754, all spouses were required on marriage to sign the parish register, or to make a mark if they were unable to sign. After 1839, moreover, the statistics from marriage registers were collected and published annually by the Registrar General of Births, Deaths and Marriages. The use of signatures as evidence of the extent of literacy has often been questioned, but Stephens (1987: 3) in his major survey argues that although it provides only 'a crude and imperfect yardstick', such evidence constitutes 'a valuable measure of the maximum numbers able to write'. Evidence is fragmentary and often misleading before this time, but still allows tentative estimates both of general levels and of differences between localities and genders (Stone 1969; Stephens 1987: esp. Chapter 1). As far as the period 1830–70 is concerned, Stephens (1987: 264) argues that the 'reservoir of evidence' based on census material and on the Annual Reports of the Registrar General of Births, Deaths and Marriages is 'enormous'.

Vincent (1989) extends the range of this kind of study, both by attempting to relate 'the often discrete categories of education, family, work, popular beliefs, the imagination and politics', and by integrating statistical evidence with 'the many forms of literary evidence' (p. xi). Like Stephens, Vincent makes extensive use of marriage registers as his principal source of statistical evidence. However, assessing the uses to which this literacy was put, and the nature of functional literacy in a rapidly changing society, demands a wider range of sources. In particular, Vincent utilizes evidence from working-class autobiographies as a complementary means of exploring the application of reading and writing in the distinct areas of the family, the classroom, the workplace, the response to the natural world, the imaginative life of the community and the political ideology and movements of the period 1750–1914.

A further detailed study of the rise of literacy in Victorian England (Mitch 1992) again uses marriage signatures as the prime source of quantitative evidence. Mitch goes on, however, to try to determine the relative importance of popular demand as compared with public policy in the spread of mass literacy. To do this, he attempts to develop a cost–benefit analysis of whether it was worthwhile for working-class families and individuals to become literate. He calculates, for example, the value of acquiring literacy in terms of tuition costs and opportunity costs, and sets these factors against the potential benefits of acquiring literacy. These calculations again involve making use of a wider range of sources than marriage registers alone.

which oral history was related to educational issues. First, he noted, much of this early work had been undertaken by historians interested in wider questions of social class, family, local community structures or ethnic history. They therefore treated only incidentally 'educational issues such as schooling, growing up, acculturation', and tended to concentrate mainly on working-class children's 'preparation for work and industrial training' (Spaull 1988: 76). Second, he found that radical labour historians, who were drawing increasingly on oral history, encountered 'theoretical ambiguities' in working with school teachers, specifically over how to categorize them in terms of their social class. Third, Spaull argued that a spread in the use of oral history would be hindered as far as the history of education was concerned by the principal focus of the field on nineteenth-century schooling and a preference for quantitative sources. However, he predicted, 'as studies of schooling and social class edge towards the twentieth century, the availability of oral sources will add new research dimensions to the history of education' (1988: 76). This prediction was soon borne out, and indeed the use of oral history techniques in relation to education has been stimulated further by the development of two major critiques of the problems of documentary sources.

The first of these critiques is that documentary sources portray a top-down view of the history of education, and take for granted inbuilt power balances. They record in the main the dominant views and assumptions of policy makers and administrators. Therefore, according to such an argument, they lead us to view educational history through the eyes of the 'winners' of conflicts over the nature and purposes of education (see also Silver 1983). These winners or survivors are characterized as mainly middle class, male and white. Smelser (1991), in his study of British working-class education in the nineteenth century, notes that the nature of the sources constitutes a 'recurrent and inevitable difficulty' (p. 5). This is because, as he suggests, 'Most of the things recorded about the working classes were written by representatives of other classes. This occurs in all societies, by virtue of the unequal distribution of literacy, power, wealth, and access to authorship.' Therefore, according to Smelser, 'Methodologically this behoves historians to consult sources produced by representatives of those classes themselves and perhaps to distrust sources produced by others' (pp. 5–6). However, Smelser (p. 6) also warns against interpreting this principle too narrowly, which he contends can lead to biases of its own:

> This intellectual position has served as a useful methodological corrective to naïve interpretations of evidently biased materials. It should not, however, be pressed so far as to deny that any social group both makes its history and has it made for it by other groups. In addition, biases inhere in the other alternatives. For example, studies of working-class biographies are obviously skewed as sources toward the more literate – and, in all likelihood, the higher – levels of that class.

Overall, Smelser concludes, 'The problem of the reliability of different historical sources does not admit of any definitive solution, but rather invites a practical and sceptical approach to all of them.'

Caution in accepting at face value the documents left behind by dominant social groups extends similarly to historical discussion of education for girls, women and ethnic minorities. In some cultural contexts powerful colonial interests may also be held to have suppressed the culture of indigenous people. In general, it is often proposed, documentary sources tend to exclude or marginalize the losers, especially the working class, women and ethnic minorities and indigenous peoples. Oral sources are presented as a suitable means of discovering the experiences, outlooks and alternative agendas of such groups.

Stephen Humphries (1981), for example, seeks to explore the world of working-class childhood and youth in England from 1889 to 1939. He argues that working-class children and youth tried to resist the structures imposed upon them by a hegemonic dominant culture, and portrays them not as 'hooligans', as they were often perceived in official documents, but as 'rebels'. In order to understand the nature of their 'resistance', which he argues is 'under-recorded and under-researched', he prefers oral to documentary sources. According to Humphries (1981: 3),

> Clearly, any account of an under-privileged and largely anonymous group like working-class youth requires a methodological approach different from that ordinarily employed by historians. Since the control of manuscript and printed evidence by adults (normally middle-class adults) is absolute, most documentary sources present a biased and distorted view of the resistance of working-class youth. This book will

attempt to redress this balance by rewriting the history of working-class childhood and youth largely in the words of working-class people who themselves experienced it between 1889 and 1939; official accounts of disruptive and delinquent behaviour will be assessed in the light of their reminiscences.

Oral history, he insists, 'offers a viable method of placing this class resistance back at the centre of analysis' (p. 27). In particular, interviews illuminate 'the precise circumstances and consequences of opposition to school authority because official records often distort the motives and underestimate the frequency of children's resistance' (p. 29). In order to redress the balance, he concludes, 'we must listen to the testimony of those old working-class people who stood accused in the official records of acts of resistance against rational state instruction' (p. 29). However, it is also worth noting that Humphries's emphasis on the idea of 'resistance' has itself been challenged by other historians, who note a high level of acquiescence and even of positive endorsement for working-class schools from many memoirs and oral sources relating to this period (see Rose 1993).

Timutimu *et al.* (1998) also focus on the problems raised by documentary evidence. In this case they argue that the history of education in New Zealand/Aotearoa has been written in the main by pakehas (Europeans and colonists) rather than by the Maori indigenous people: 'Up until this stage almost all the research on the Native Schools has been conducted by Pakeha academics and based primarily upon the reports and other writings of officials of the Department of Education. Thus, the voices of Maori – those most affected by the Native Schools – have had virtually no place in these accounts' (p. 113). Indeed, they contend (p. 118), 'Pakeha research and publications concerning Maori knowledge and Maori experience are often treated with scepticism by Maori.' In order to recover the 'previously silenced or muted voices of former pupils and teachers of Native Schools' (p. 114), they make use of oral testimonies. These they regard as complementary to documentary sources: 'Our concern to gather the oral histories of former teachers and pupils, therefore, does not mean that we are privileging oral accounts over those drawn from official and other documentary sources. Rather, we see these different types of historical data as complementary – informing and providing insights into each other' (p. 114).

The second major critique of documentary sources and methods – and a corollary of the first – is that they provide too little penetration into the classroom, the learning context or the interface between teachers and learners. The suggestion here is that historical research has tended not to be about educational processes as such, but rather about policy, administration and institutions. Goodson, for example, has suggested that documentary sources have encouraged an approach to the history of education that is overly concerned with 'Acts and facts'. Sources such as government records, according to Goodson (1988: 5), 'offer limited help in reconstructing the detail of schooling'. In order to understand more clearly the evolution of the school curriculum, for example, different sources and methods would be required, including life-history method applied to teachers (Goodson 1994).

In examining the history of teachers' professional practice, Gardner and Cunningham (1997) emphasize that it is necessary to employ the oral history interview as their 'principal methodological tool' (p. 331). They suggest that oral history holds 'unique promise' for conceptualizing research questions and for methodological design (p. 332). They point out the potential problems involved in this approach: 'Engagement with data produced by the agency of memory and dialogue presents us with enormous challenges, as well as great promise' (p. 340). Nevertheless, they insist, 'if we can use such data carefully and creatively alongside our more familiar documentary sources, then we may be able to go beyond histories which are locked into unitary paradigms . . . and look for more challenging ways of rethinking the problem of structure and agency' (p. 340).

Gardner's oral history research on the use of corporal punishment by teachers in English working-class elementary schools in the 1920s (Gardner 1996) illustrates these issues further in developing a distinction between teacher accounts and pupil or student accounts. Gardner acknowledges several practical difficulties involved in interviewing former teachers; for example, the relatively smaller number of teachers compared with their pupils, their relatively greater age and the sensitivity of the topic, as well as the generally distorting effects of memory. On the other hand, he argues, 'The memories of such individuals promise a source of intimate and detailed information capable both of refining the bland messages inscribed in the official documents and tempering the pained, passionate classroom recollections of former pupils' (p. 144). The conclusions from his research based on these teacher accounts suggest that corporal punishment was 'a more prominent part of classroom life than the documentary record can ever admit', but was at the same time not as universal, intensive or uncontrolled as might be implied in pupil recollections such as those studied by Humphries (1981).

Other recent research, however, suggests that it is possible to use documentary sources equally effectively in the exploration of such issues. Purvis's research on working-class women in nineteenth-century England, for example, makes suggestive use of documentary sources (Purvis 1989b), although she is aware of the problematic nature of this kind of evidence (see especially Purvis 1985). In Australia, Marjorie Theobald has pursued the possibilities of documentary research in relation to the history of women's education in interesting new ways. For example, she has reconstructed the lives of women teachers (Theobald 1996: esp. Chapter 6) and educational administrators (Theobald 2000) from detailed bureaucratic records, often demonstrating what she calls 'the burgeoning capacities of the educational state to contest the meanings of female sexuality' (1996: 203). Meanwhile, researchers such as Cuban (1993) and Finkelstein (1989, 1998), in the United States, have drawn on a wide range of documentary sources to illuminate the world of the classroom and the underlying constancy of pedagogy in American schools.

More broadly, the kinds of study discussed in this section suggest the potential value of combining different kinds of source or method to help understanding of historical problems. The use of ethnographic methods, for example, can complement the analysis of documentary sources to provide not only confirmation or triangulation of results, but also an extension of the research project itself to include new and different questions (see, for example, Smith *et al.* 1988). Similarly, interviews with current or retired teachers or policy makers can, in combination with documentary evidence, shed interesting light on change in education over the longer term. A case in point is current research that investigates teachers' ideas about their own 'professionalism', alongside published and unpublished documentary evidence concerning the changing nature of ideas about teacher professionalism over the past 50 years (McCulloch *et al.* 2000; in relation to interviewing educational policy makers see, for example, Ozga and Gewirtz 1994).

Each of these kinds of study, then, offers the potential of a methodological pluralism in research that can greatly extend our historical knowledge and understanding of education, albeit that they are indicative of the concentration of the field on the comparatively recent past. In an important sense, this development is a logical corollary to the widening range of social theories applied to the history of education, and the new disciplinary and interdisciplinary approaches to the field that we reviewed in Chapter 4. The application of particular methods must always be informed by the research question that is being addressed. The use of more than one method can address not only more complex issues, but also a wide range of social scientific, historical and educational concerns. In the final chapter we return to these questions of theory and method in order to inform our discussion of the design of historical research projects in education.

7 | Designing and carrying out a research project

In this book we have sought to bring together a very large and widely scattered literature on general historiography and the history of education, including material on aims, methods and new avenues of enquiry. In the absence of a similar volume we have considered it important also to provide a genealogy of the current field, illustrating its relation to antecedents in 'history' and 'education', and to cousins in the social sciences. At the same time we have given considerable space to the raw materials available for the historical study of education and how these can be utilized by researchers. Our purpose in this respect has been to indicate some of the specific characteristics of such sources rather than to devote space to a general discussion of historical method. Readers wishing to engage with this wider literature are directed to our recommendations for further reading at the end of this chapter.

In this final chapter we bring together a set of considerations that have arisen in the course of this book concerning the design and execution of historical research projects in education. We do not intend to generate a list of specific topics that deserve to be researched or further developed, partly because there are so many possible themes available that to attempt a list might be both arbitrary and exclusionary, and partly because we believe it to be appropriate for individuals to assess the possibilities for research in the light of their own background, skills and interests. Instead, we seek here to provide a more general rationale and prospectus for research projects in this area that can be applied discriminatingly in each particular case. Nor do we wish to suggest that our ideas offer the final word on the subject: designing and carrying out historical research in education involves wrestling with a range of issues to which there is often no right or simple answer. This chapter should therefore be read not so much as a conclusion, but as a starting point for the difficult business of locating, developing and refining your own area of research interest.

Problems and opportunities for study

In our discussion in Chapters 2, 3 and 4 we pointed to a range of conceptual problems and opportunities that confront those undertaking historical study in education, whether they be experienced historians embarking on a fresh project, seasoned educational and social researchers unused to historical method or novices to either tradition. Then, in Chapters 5 and 6, we pointed to some of the problems and opportunities afforded by the historical sources available. In the following pages we summarize these problems and opportunities.

Problems

Problem 1: Competing purposes

For much of this century historians and educationists have been unable to agree on the purpose of their work. This pervasive disagreement can be summarized as the 'long-standing and defining difference between the practice . . . of academic historians who reconstruct the past in ways influenced by present concerns and of educationists who invoke the past in order to apply its lessons to present concerns' (Richardson 1999b: 138). Put another way, this is a clash of outlook between scholars who seek to study the past for its own sake (albeit through a contemporary lens) and those who start from the issues of the day in order to uncover the lessons of a 'usable past'.

More generally, there is a distinction in practice between the characteristic working methods of historians and social researchers. This is the emphasis given by historians to sources which record sets of events in a chronology that can be reconstructed contrasted with the emphasis given by social researchers to procedures from which theories of social action and structure, fixed often uncertainly in time, may be refined or freshly constructed. Nevertheless, this practical distinction is not a theoretical necessity and many of the studies we discussed in Chapter 4 and the last part of Chapter 6 explore the extent to which historians and social scientists are, in fact, interested in the same things. Perhaps the key point here is the obligation this suggests for researchers to be clear about their intentions, how these relate to method and how both are presented. We return to this point in detail below.

Problem 2: Preferred themes and competing audiences

This question is linked to the first. It has been a problem generally in so far as the rival research traditions just described have fragmented the field as a whole and helped to reduce its influence. It remains a specific problem for educationists in that academic historians in the UK and the USA have demonstrated in recent decades the political and cultural power of their critiques of historically oriented educational studies.

Over the past 30 years academic historians in the UK have penetrated a field that had formerly been left mainly to educationists. In the process they have expanded it and redefined many of its key issues on their own terms and with reference to their preferred themes: education and economic change; the universities and elites; children's work and welfare; technical and scientific education; childhood in English society (Richardson 1999b: 134). For this authorship the concept of audience is relatively unproblematic. Study guide series such as *New Studies in Economic and Social History* introduce 'key themes' in education to history undergraduates and postgraduates; a modest flow of doctoral theses and monographs results; education is incorporated – sometimes with powerful political results (for example, Wiener 1981; Barnett 1986) – into historical works aimed at a general readership.

In a parallel development educational studies in the English-speaking world has now largely abandoned its former allegiance to the humanities, turning itself into what is now broadly an ahistorical field dominated by the fieldwork methods and techniques of 'social research' and the scientific procedures of experimental psychology. The 'revisionist' historiographical wave of the 1960s and 1970s, concerned though it was to promote social history and its relation to social theory, ironically did much to assist this development in that it pilloried the old history of education taught to teacher trainees and written by 'insiders'. Important too has been a lessening political confidence internationally in the social and economic efficiency of education, leading to the squeezing of all educational research which cannot demonstrate direct relevance to policy imperatives. However, this problem may now be turning into an opportunity as social researchers in education become increasingly disillusioned with the explanatory power of present-centred research problems (see below).

Problem 3: Lack of historical training among educational and social researchers

One effect in the UK of the politicization of education just outlined has been a return over the past two decades to the conditions of 1900–60, when very few educationists had any formal training in history. Thus, even though there is currently evidence of a reawakening of interest in historically orientated research methods such as 'life history' and 'oral history', this has brought with it specific problems associated with a blurring of the boundaries between formerly discrete methodological traditions in history and sociology. These dangers are: a lack of clarity about methodology and the role of competing source materials; the forcing or selection of evidence to fit *a priori* concepts or theories, as if using historical sources to test a hypothesis scientifically; and a tendency to foster uncritical assumptions and ahistorical conclusions.

Carl Kaestle (1988: 68–70) has summarized these problems in the context of educational history as the tendency of the inexperienced researcher to:

- confuse correlations and associations with causes;
- be inaccurate in defining key terms, especially through vagueness or 'presentism' (the danger of assuming that terms had their present-day connotations in the past, which is a form of anachronism);
- fail to keep clear a distinction between evidence of ideas about how people should behave and evidence of how ordinary people in fact behaved;
- fail to distinguish between intent and consequences and fall into the trap of inferring the former from the latter.

To be sure, these are all difficulties with which academic historians wrestle routinely. The specific challenge for historical research conducted by educationists is twofold. First the political nature of education in the present makes them specifically vulnerable to each of the problems raised by Kaestle. Second, the rise of quasi-historical methods of social research brings with it the danger that social researchers new to such methods – and the documentary sources which support them – will underestimate the complexity of the problems Kaestle identifies.

Problem 4: Academic historians in the educational domain

If most educationists and social researchers lack formal historical training, a problem that faces academic historians is how to comprehend the characteristic problems of the educational domain or address the questions that are raised by educational practice. Most academic historians lack direct expertise in this area, and are limited in their professional experience to universities which then become the prime source of their educational expertise and insight. Further, it may be argued that many historians are somewhat narrow in their specialist interests and preferred techniques when compared with educational and social researchers, who are often called upon to work and engage within a range of disciplines and methods.

Problem 5: The telescoping of the past

The problem here lies in looking the wrong way through the telescope, so that the past is conceived as two broad categories: recent and contemporary history, which is accessible and 'relevant' (from, say, 1850 or 1950 or even 1980 to the present); and everything before, which is esoteric and remote. This is a general trend that is afflicting teaching (although not research) in academic history but is especially prevalent in the historical research of educationists. The influence over the field of sociology is one cause, encouraging many researchers in the belief that the only worthwhile history of education is that after the onset of mass industrialization. Another cause is the increasing interest shown recently by politicians in education which can mean that research funding is defined in relation to the interests of the modern nation state. Telescoping of the past in another sense can also create a kind of tunnel vision in which only one trend is evident, stretching back through the years and culminating in the present. Both such approaches to the past are a recipe for myopia and distorted vision.

Problem 6: Selecting a viable project

This problem is generic in historical studies, especially where a project is reliant on sufficient evidence being forthcoming from unpublished sources in archives whose content cannot even be guessed at in advance. In the study of history the limitations that arise are usually connected to the viability of the historical sources available – their existence at all or the extent to which they are substantial enough to bear the weight of a rigorous research project. Students and experienced researchers new to historical study need to be aware of this danger and to make an assessment of risk at an early stage in projects of this kind.

Opportunities

To be set against these undoubted problems are the opportunities available to those undertaking historical study of education, most of which directly counterbalance the difficulties just discussed.

Opportunity 1: Historical writing and the lay audience

It is undoubtedly the case in Britain that the threat to their discipline of the early 1980s has led leading academic historians to concentrate ever more clearly on the need to reach both specialized and lay audiences (see, for example, Cannadine 1987). The work of Martin Wiener (1981) and Correlli Barnett (1986) on the history of English education has shown the spectacular impact that can be made by such subject matter on contemporary politics and cultural attitudes more widely. This has been so even when, as in Wiener's case, the historical method deployed has been criticized as unconvincing (see Raven 1989).

This is a lesson which those in the sphere of educational studies have found difficult to emulate. This in part is owing to the poor quality of writing characteristic of much educational research. Historical studies of education can be well written, subtly wrought and appealing to a lay audience at a time when much educational research is belittled for its lack of ambition or turgid, abstruse presentation. Within a general collection of educational research, a good historical study can shine as an aesthetic, crafted artefact. Even short works on modest themes can appeal well beyond a strictly professional audience. Larger monographs on more complex themes demand for their construction considerable intellectual qualities of their authors; however, when these qualities are combined with a general intelligence in presentation and interpretation the prize is a work of durable cultural and political influence.

Opportunity 2: Freedom of enquiry

Following from the previous theme, historical study can be uniquely reward-ing for both author and reader, in that it takes as its subject matter any material evidence – written, printed, visual, statistical and oral – within a given period that might illuminate its theme. As such, the intellectual demands are great, but so, too, is the reward of fashioning a lasting text, rich in its analytical perspectives, broad in its vision and subtle in its presen-tation. As Kaestle (1988: 71) has remarked,

> historians have always been scavengers. Since history involves all human experience and thought, historians have constantly raided other disciplines for new techniques of analysis and new insights into society and human nature. This helps explain why there is no single methodol-ogy in history and why historians love their craft so much: because it is so complex and so all-embracing.

Opportunity 3: History as a practical subject

A further considerable gain for both the author and the reader of historical studies of education lies in the opportunity they offer to ponder the nature of continuity and change in education and the societies with which it inter-acts. This core task of the historian – to elucidate both the turning points and points that failed to turn in history – serves also to illuminate the possi-bilities for action and understanding in the present. Such pragmatic ends are often seen as more the concern of educationists with their accountability to a broad professional audience than of the academic historian, but this is not necessarily so.

Moreover, a practical dimension to historical research exists regardless of the period under study. It is a fallacy to believe that the more remote is a period of study in the past the less 'relevant' is the enquiry: since the fourth century BC at least, the conduct of education in society has been a central, speculative part of European thought. Certainly, the study of education in periods before AD 1750 requires particular imaginative powers and a wide familiarity with contemporary sources, whose acquisition is time consum-ing, but the wider the chronology the greater and more profound can be the perspective provided on our present concerns. The same holds true for comparative, cross-cultural and international historical studies in which the spatial context may be as immense as that of time.

Opportunity 4: Contribution to educational studies

No less attractive is the point that an increased historical understanding of education can illuminate the possibilities for effective educational research as a whole, both in the present and in the future. At a time when education-ists are beleaguered in the face of government policies and programmes which are often anti-intellectual and increasingly instrumental, there is much to be gained from a clear-sighted reconstruction of the historical relationships between current educational controversies, their roots and their antecedents. Here is a sphere of historical research that is of great practical interest and potential. Support for such an approach can be found in many quarters. For example, the British government policy document *Excellence in Schools* asserted in 1997 that the difficulties that confronted the education system had 'deep and historic roots' (Department for Education and Employment 1997: 10). The onus is on researchers to trace as carefully as possible the nature of these 'roots'. The Chief Inspector of Schools, again in Britain, while generally denigrating the value of educational research, has emphasized the potential benefits of historical research, asserting that 'the future lies, if it lies anywhere, in the rediscovery of the importance of historical perspective . . . and above all, in a return to what was once the classical terrain: issues, that is, concerning social class and educability and schools as social systems' (Woodhead 1998). Finally, we may add that if educationists wish to understand better the causes of their denigration by contemporary politicians an important starting point is a full reconstruction of the history of educational research in the era of state education systems. This is an undertaking which is barely at the outline stage of development.

Opportunity 5: The promise of interdisciplinary enquiry
Throughout this book, but in Chapter 4 especially, we have tried to show how historical research and the perspective it generates can both contribute to and benefit from an engagement with other research traditions, and that such an engagement is becoming more common as social researchers are turning to the past in increasing numbers.

Although welcome and full of potential, this development begs major questions of researchers undertaking such studies. In particular it requires them to be mindful of the judgements they must make *as historians*, whatever their other intellectual allegiances. It is as well to pose the questions that accompany such judgements at the outset of any historical research project in education *and* to review the provisional answers as the work progresses.

- What is the research question to be addressed? How does it relate to the findings of earlier historical research and how will it extend knowledge and understanding of the field as a whole?
- How clear are the organizing ideas and presuppositions that underlie the research question and the means used to explore it?
- What should be the boundaries – chronological and conceptual – that define the project? How 'do-able' is the project in the time available with the skills and resources at your disposal, and to what level of sophistication?
- What are the working tools – historical sources, analytical constructs and

research techniques – best matched to the objects of enquiry? What practical problems do these raise in terms of access, expense and difficulties of fieldwork and interpretation of data?

- Is the project designed primarily to illustrate and amplify a theory or hypothesis, or is it intended to establish a set of specific events and experiences in the past from which a broader theory or hypothesis might be inferred (by the author or others)?
- In the proposed project, what would count as critical engagement with theory as opposed to the uncritical application of theory to the period and theme under investigation?
- If a social theory or model is to be deployed as a substantive part of the analysis, how is it to be contextualized in time and place? How is the impact on the theory or model of such a contextualization to be assessed?
- In studies concerned with the recent past that draw on the fieldwork techniques of social research, what are the ethics of reporting? Are there any grounds for departing from the conventions of academic history by failing to identify specific individuals or institutions? If so, what are these?
- Finally, how plausible is the explanation or interpretation of the research question and what means, if any, are available to validate the conclusions of the project? If the study is of a particular case, can general conclusions be drawn and, if so, on what basis?

Conclusions

The opportunities that we have just outlined may be grasped by individual researchers or by groups working in a wide range of circumstances, including the three main kinds of readers whom we identified in Chapter 1 as the audiences for this book. The key point, perhaps, is for all researchers to start from and build on their own experience and interests, with the aim of informing and deepening their historical insight. In the case of our first audience, trained historians new to the study of education, this may entail deploying familiar skills of archival research in relation to unaccustomed concepts and debates derived from the social sciences in general and educational studies in particular. In the case of social researchers new to historical methods, it may suggest a theoretical basis for a project, starting out from a detailed reading of a particular social theorist or group of thinkers, coupled with a desire to subject the ideas raised to the contexts of time and place. For our third audience, practising educationists, a beginning may arise from practical experience in and understanding of a contemporary educational setting, such as a school, college or workplace, and a curiosity to explore it in a historical perspective. In each case difficult conceptual and methodological challenges may well arise in the course of the research. In the face of such a challenge it is important to be realistic about what can be achieved; to set ambitious goals where feasible and necessary, but to be sure at the same time that the project is manageable to the extent that it can be tackled successfully in the time available. Identifying the strengths and weaknesses of other research studies from these various perspectives may itself help in defining one's own project, with the aim of complementing existing work in an area that is of special concern and particularly accessible for you.

Equally important, in the light of these varying motivations, is selecting among the different kinds of project design available, each with its potential pitfalls for the historical researcher in education.

- The *contextualizing* study: projects that confine their historical dimension to an introductory chapter before focusing in depth on a contemporary problem. In such a case, what degree of immersion in the available sources is appropriate for the historical section of the project? In what way does this section develop pertinent themes and issues and relate these to the rest of the project? How can the researcher avoid the characteristic problems of anachronism and telescoping of the past that so often afflict such studies?
- The *single-method* study: detailed investigations of specific historical problems relying primarily on one kind of source or type of evidence. For such a project, to what extent can the mass of evidence or data available from the predominant source generate adequate explanations or interpretations in answer to the research question? What theoretical, ethical and practical difficulties lie in the way of recovering and presenting this evidence?
- The *interdisciplinary* study: projects that deploy different kinds of research methodology and evidence in a complementary fashion to investigate a particular historical problem. In such a case, how can these different strands best be related to each other? What are the distinctive theoretical, ethical and practical problems involved in each element of the research and how can these be reconciled to form an integrated whole?

Each of these kinds of project, as we have witnessed at various stages in this book, holds its own dangers and inherent difficulties, but each in its own way also holds much of potential value for historians, educationists and social researchers alike.

This in turn leads us to sum up the overarching opportunities of this field of research. Whatever the strengths and weaknesses, background and interests of individual researchers, a broad project of historical research in education exists that offers exciting potential and wide scope. In the process of cultivating this field, the boundaries that have fragmented and undermined it in the past may be erased or at least become less marked. The opportunity exists for historical research in education to develop into a major interest for historians and educationists alike, rather than being of marginal concern to both groups. At the same time, interdisciplinary and theoretical research rooted in the wider social sciences is already suggesting important new directions for study in the years ahead.

Further reading

The following is a short list of suggested reading which develops further the main themes raised in this book. Clearly, it is highly selective of a large literature and we have not tried to represent specific areas of historical research. Instead we have chosen works that offer an initial means of finding a way into the vast range of published works available.

Abrams, P. (1982) *Historical Sociology*. New York: Cornell University Press. A fertile discussion of the interrelated methods and interests of history and sociology. Addresses in detail the place of social theory in historical interpretation.

Caspard, P. (ed.) (1995) *International Guide for Research in the History of Education*, 2nd edn. London: Peter Lang. Provides details of national societies, key works and leading individuals in the field.

Cohen, S. (1976) The history of the history of education, 1900–1976: uses of the past, *Harvard Educational Review*, 46(3): 298–330. Reviews the historiographical development of the field in the USA from 1900 to the mid-1970s. Emphasizes the institutional contexts within which the history of education has been generated.

Crook, D. and Aldrich, R. (eds) (2000) *History of Education for the 21st Century*. London: Institute of Education. A set of essays reflecting on current developments and future prospects for the field in Britain.

Gall, M. D., Borg, W. R. and Gall, J. P. (1996) *Educational Research: an Introduction*, 6th edn. New York: Longman. A good, recent introduction to the methods and techniques of historical research in education. Critical and balanced. Provides American and Japanese case studies.

Kaestle, C. F. (1988) Recent methodological developments in the history of American education, in R. M. Jaeger (ed.) *Complementary Methods for Research in Education*. Washington, DC: American Educational Research Association, pp. 61–71. An accomplished and concise statement of the aims and methods of 'revisionist' history of education in the USA. Still being republished in current compendia.

Lowe, R. (ed.) (2000) *History of Education: Major Themes*. London: Routledge. A four-volume international collection of 111 contributions on different topics in this field over the past 30 years.

Richardson, W. (1999) Historians and educationists: the history of education as a field of study in post-war England. Part I: 1945–1972; Part II: 1972–1996, *History of Education*, 28(1): 1–30; 28(2): 109–41. A similar treatment to that of Cohen, concentrating on the development of the field in England since 1945.

Tosh, J. (2000) *The Pursuit of History*. London: Longman. An outstanding general introduction to the study of modern history. Accessible, challenging and up to date, with a very useful and discriminating guide to further reading.

Glossary

Ahistorical: an account of human affairs in which **context** or **chronology** is vague or absent (*see also* **Unhistorical**).

Anachronism: the error of assigning a concept, term or event outside its chronological context.

Artefacts: remains as opposed to records; for example, school desks, educational equipment, buildings.

Chronology: a record of a sequence of events in the order that they took place.

Context: events and issues located in relation to their time and place.

Continuity: the extent to which problems, institutions etc. remain recognizably the same over a period of time.

Documentary sources: manuscripts and printed matter of all kinds.

Educationists: those concerned to understand and improve education.

Historians: those whose prime concern is the reconstruction of the past.

Historical sociology: a branch of sociology mainly concerned with exploring **social theory(ies)** over time.

Historiography: the theory and practice of historical enquiry and writing.

Life history: an emerging branch of social research in which biography is related to **social theory**.

Narrative research: study and writing which gives priority to **chronology**.

Oral history: a method of historical research which creates and utilizes **oral sources**.

Oral sources: recordings or transcripts derived from interviews.

Present-mindedness/Presentism: the danger of assuming that a term had its present day meaning or connotation in the past (*see also* **Anachronism**).

Primary sources: first-hand accounts produced by those involved in or witness to a particular historical episode.

Revisionism: new approaches to the understanding of a particular historical episode or a general view of the past.

Secondary sources: interpretative accounts of historical episodes produced at a remove.

Social theory: theory about the nature, relationships and dynamics of society.

Unhistorical: a historical claim or inference which is misinformed or anachronistic (*see also* **Ahistorical**).

Visual sources: paintings, photographs, cinematic, televisual.

Whiggish/Whig interpretation of history: a term now mainly used pejoratively, describing forms of historical enquiry which assume progress in human affairs.

References

Abbott, M. (ed.) (1996) *History Skills: A Student's Handbook*. London: Routledge.

Abbs, P. (1974) *Autobiography in Education*. London: Heinemann.

Abrams, P. (1982) *Historical Sociology*. Ithaca, NY: Cornell University Press.

Alcorn, N. (1999) 'To the Fullest Extent of His Powers': C. E. Beeby's Life in Education. Wellington: Victoria University Press.

Aldcroft, D. (1992) *Education, Training and Economic Performance 1944 to 1990*. Manchester: Manchester University Press.

Aldcroft, D. (1998) Education and development: the experience of rich and poor nations, *History of Education*, 27(3): 235–54.

Aldrich, R. (1982) *An Introduction to the History of Education*. London: Hodder and Stoughton.

Aldrich, R. and Gordon, P. (eds) (1989) *Dictionary of British Educationists*. London: Woburn.

Althusser, L. (1972) Ideology and ideological state apparatuses, in B. R. Cosin (ed.) *Education: Structure and Society*. Buckingham: Open University Press, pp. 242–80.

Anderson, C. A. and Bowman, M. (1976) Education and economic modernisation in historical perspective, in Stone (ed.) *op. cit.*, pp. 3–19.

Anderson, G. (1990) *Fundamentals of Educational Research*. London: Falmer (2nd edn 1998).

Andrew, A. (1985) In pursuit of the past: some problems in the collection, analysis and use of historical documentary evidence, in Burgess (ed.) *op. cit.*, pp. 91–131.

Apple, M. (1986) *Teachers and Texts: A Political Economy of Class and Gender Relations in Education*. London: RKP.

Archer, M. (1979) *Social Origins of Educational Systems*. London: Sage.

Archer, R. L. (1921) *Secondary Education in the Nineteenth Century*. Cambridge: Cambridge University Press.

Argles, M. (1971) *British Government Publications in Education During the Nineteenth Century*. Leicester: History of Education Society.

Argles, M. and Vaughan, J. A. (1982) *British Government Publications Concerning Education During the Twentieth Century*, 4th edn. Leicester: History of Education Society.

Aries, P. (1960) *Centuries of Childhood*. London: Penguin.

Armytage, W. H. G. (1953) The place of the history of education in training courses for teachers, *British Journal of Educational Studies*, 1: 114–20.

Armytage, W. H. G. (1964) *Four Hundred Years of English Education*. Cambridge: Cambridge University Press.

Asher, J. W. (1976) *Educational Research and Evaluation Methods*. Boston: Little Brown and Co.

Atkinson, P., Davies, B. and Delamont, S. (eds) (1995) *Discourse and Reproduction*. Cresskill, NJ: Hampton Press.

Bailyn, B. (1960) *Education in the Forming of American Society*. Chapel Hill, NC: University of North Carolina Press.

Bailyn, B. (1963) Education as a discipline: some historical notes, in J. Walton and J. L. Kuethe (eds) *The Discipline of Education*. Madison, WI: University of Wisconsin Press, pp. 125–39.

Baker, D. and Harrigan, P. (1980) *The Making of Frenchmen: Current Directions in the History of Education in France, 1679–1979*. Waterloo, Ont.: Historical Reflections Press.

Baker, K. (1993) *The Turbulent Years: My Life in Politics*. London: Faber and Faber.

Ball, S. (1981) *Beachside Comprehensive: A Case-study of Secondary Schooling*. Cambridge: Cambridge University Press.

Ball, S. (ed.) (1990) *Foucault and Education: Disciplines and Knowledge*. London: Routledge.

Banks, J. A. (1989) From universal history to historical sociology, *British Journal of Sociology*, 40(4): 521–43.

Banks, O. (1955) *Parity and Prestige in English Secondary Education*. London: RKP.

Barber, M. (1994) *The Making of the 1944 Education Act*. London: Cassell.

Barnard, H. C. (1947) *A History of English Education from 1769*. London: University of London Press (2nd edn 1961).

Barnett, C. (1986) *The Audit of War: The Illusion and Reality of Britain as a Great Nation*. London: Macmillan.

Baron, S., Finn, D., Grant, N., Green, M. and Johnson, R. (1982) Silver foils: a reply, *British Journal of Sociology of Education*, 3(2): 189–97.

Barzun, J. and Graff, H. (1957) *The Modern Researcher*. New York: Harcourt, Brace and World (5th edn 1992).

Bassey, M. (1992) Creating education through research, *British Educational Research Journal*, 18(1): 3–16.

Bassey, M. (1995) *Creating Education Through Research: A Global Perspective of Educational Research for the Twenty-first Century*. Newark: Kirklington Moor Press/BERA.

Bentley, M. (ed.) (1997) *Companion to Historiography*. London: Routledge.

Bernbaum, G. (1971) Sociological techniques and historical study, in History of Education Society (ed.) *History, Sociology and Education*. Leicester: History of Education Society.

Bernstein, B. (1997) Class and pedagogies: visible and invisible, in A. H. Halsey, H. Lauder, P. Brown, A. S. Wells (eds) *Education: Culture, Economy, Society*. Oxford: Oxford University Press, pp. 59–79.

Best, J. (ed.) (1983) *Historical Enquiry in Education: A Research Agenda*. Washington, DC: American Educational Research Association.

Betts, R. (1981) The school desk in the nineteenth century, *History of Education Society Bulletin*, 27: 24–35.

Birmingham, D. (1997) History in Africa, in Bentley (ed.) *op. cit.*, pp. 692–708.

Black, J. and Macraild, D. (1997) *Studying History*. London: Macmillan.

Blishen, E. (1955) *Roaring Boys: A Schoolmaster's Agony*. London: Thames and Hudson.

Board of Education (1938) *Secondary Education with Special Reference to Grammar Schools and Technical High Schools* (Spens Report). London: HMSO.

Board of Education (1943) *Curriculum and Examinations in Secondary Schools* (Norwood Report). London: HMSO.

Bourdieu, P. and Passeron, J. C. (1977) *Reproduction in Education, Society and Culture*. London: Sage.

Bourke, J. (1998) Housewifery in working-class England, 1860–1919, in P. Sharpe (ed.) *Women's Work: The English Experience 1650–1914*. London: Arnold, pp. 332–58.

Bourne, J. M. (1986) History at the universities, *History*, 71: 54–60.

Bowles, S. and Gintis, H. (1976) *Schooling in Capitalist America: Educational Reform and the Contradictions of Economic Life*. London: RKP.

Brehony, K. (1998) 'Even far distant Japan' is 'showing an interest': the English Froebel movement's turn to Sloyd, *History of Education*, 27(3): 279–95.

Brickman, W. W. (1949) *Guide to Research in Educational History*. New York: New York University Bookstore.

Brickman, W. W. (1964) Revisionism and the study of the history of education, *History of Education Quarterly*, 4(4): 209–23.

Briggs, A. (1967) Sociology and history, in A. T. Welford, M. Argyle, D. Glass and J. Norris (eds) *Society: Problems and Methods of Study*, rev. edn. London: Routledge and Kegan Paul.

Briggs, A. (1972) The study of the history of education, *History of Education*, 1(1): 5–22.

Brown, R. and Daniels, C. (1986) *Learning History: A Guide to Advanced Study*. London: Macmillan.

Bryant, M. (1979) *The Unexpected Revolution: A Study in the History of the Education of Women and Girls in the Nineteenth Century*. London: University of London Institute of Education.

Burgess, R. (ed.) (1985) *Strategies of Educational Research: Qualitative Methods*. London: Falmer.

Burke, P. (1980) *Sociology and History*. London: Allen & Unwin.

Burke, P. (ed.) (1991) *New Perspectives on Historical Writing*. Cambridge: Polity Press.

Burnett, J. (ed.) (1982) *Destiny Obscure: Autobiographies of Childhood, Education and Family from the 1820s to the 1920s*. London: Penguin.

Burstyn, J. (1977) Women's education in England during the nineteenth century: a review of the literature, 1970–1976, *History of Education*, 6(1): 11–19.

Burstyn, J. (1980) *Victorian Education and the Ideal of Womanhood*. London: Croom Helm.

Butler, L. (1997) History: theory and practice, in L. Butler and A. Gorst (eds) *op. cit.*, pp. 14–32.

Butler, L. and Gorst, A. (eds) (1997) *Modern British History: A Guide to Study and Research*. London: IB Tauris Publishers.

Butterfield, H. (1931) *The Whig Interpretation of History*. London: Penguin (1968 edn).

Callaghan, J. (1987) *Time and Chance*. London: Collins.

Campbell, M. (1999) The role of textuality in historical analysis, *History of Education Society Bulletin*, 63: 18–24.

Cannadine, D. (1987) British history: past, present – and future?, *Past and Present*, 116: 169–91.

Cannon, J. (ed.) (1997) *The Oxford Companion to British History*. Oxford: Oxford University Press.

Cannon, J., Davis, R., Doyle, W. and Greene, J. (eds) (1988) *The Blackwell Dictionary of Historians*. Oxford: Blackwell Reference.

Carr, E. H. (1961) *What Is History?* Harmondsworth: Penguin.

Carter, I. (1990) *Ancient Cultures of Conceit: British University Fiction in the Postwar Years*. London: Routledge.

Caunce, J. (1994) *Oral History and the Local Historian*. London: Longman.

CCCS (1981) *Unpopular Education: Schooling and Social Democracy in England since 1944*. London: Hutchinson.

Chaloner, W. H. and Richardson, R. C. (1984) *Bibliography of English Economic and Social History*. Manchester: Manchester University Press.

Charles, C. (1988) *Introduction to Educational Research*. White Plains, NY: Longman (2nd edn 1995).

Chitty, C. (1989) *Towards a New Education System: The Victory of the New Right?* London: Falmer.

Clarke, F. (1940) *Education and Social Change: An English Interpretation*. London: Sheldon Press.

Codd, J. (1988) The construction and deconstruction of educational policy documents, *Journal of Education Policy*, 3(3): 235–47.

Cohen, L. and Manion, L. (1980) *Research Methods in Education*. London: Routledge (4th edn 1994).

Cohen, R. D. (1997) The delinquents: censorship and youth culture in recent US history, *History of Education Quarterly*, 37(3): 251–70.

Cohen, S. (ed.) (1974) *Education in the United States: A Documentary History* (5 vols). New York: Random House.

Cohen, S. (1976) The history of the history of education, 1900–1976: uses of the past, *Harvard Educational Review*, 46(3): 298–330.

Coleman, B. I. (1972) The incidence of education in mid-century, in E. A. Wrigley (ed.) *Nineteenth-century Society: Essays in the Use of Quantitative Methods for the Study of Social Data*. Cambridge: Cambridge University Press, pp. 397–410.

Cook, C. (1994) *Longman Guide to Sources in Contemporary British History* (2 vols). London: Longman.

Cox, G. (1996) School music broadcasts and the BBC, 1924–47, *History of Education*, 25(44): 363–71.

Cremin, L. (1970) *American Education: the Colonial Experience 1607–1783*. New York: Harper and Row.

Cremin, L. (1980) *American Education: the National Experience, 1783–1876*. New York: Harper and Row.

Cremin, L. (1988) *American Education: the Metropolitan Experience, 1876–1980.* New York: Harper and Row.

Crook, D. (1998) Research notice board, *Bulletin of the History of Education Society,* 62: 59–60.

Crook, D. (1999) Viewing the past: the treatment of history of education on British television since 1985, *History of Education,* 28(3): 365–9.

Crowl, T. (1996) *Fundamentals of Educational Research,* 2nd edn. Madison, WI: Brown and Benchmark.

Cuban, L. (1993) *How Teachers Taught: Constancy and Change in American Classrooms 1890–1990,* 2nd edn. New York: Teachers College Press.

Cunningham, P. (1992) Teachers' professional image and the press 1950–1990, *History of Education,* 24(1): 37–56.

Curtis, B. (1989) *Building the Educational State: Canada West, 1836–1871.* London: Falmer.

Curtis, B. (1992) *True Government by Choice Men? Inspection, Education, and State Formation in Canada West.* Toronto: University of Toronto Press.

Curtis, S. J. (1948) *History of Education in Great Britain.* London: University Tutorial Press.

Dale, R. (1989) *The State and Education Policy.* Milton Keynes: Open University Press.

Davies, G. J. (1974–75) Local history studies in a college of education, *Local Historian,* 11: 395–9.

Dearing, R. (1996) *Review of Qualifications for 16–19 Year Olds: Full Report.* London: School Curriculum and Assessment Authority.

Degler, C. N. (1980) Women and the family, in Kammen (ed.) *op. cit.,* pp. 308–26.

Dekker, J. (1996) A republic of educators: educational messages in seventeenth century Dutch genre painting, *History of Education,* 36(2): 155–82.

de Landsheere, G. (1985) History of educational research, in T. Husen and N. Postlethwaite (eds) *International Encyclopedia of Education.* Oxford: Pergamon Press, 1588–97.

Department for Education (1992) *Choice and Diversity: A New Framework for Schools.* London: HMSO.

Department for Education and Employment (1997) *Excellence in Schools.* London: Stationery Office.

Donajgrodski, A. P. (ed.) (1977) *Social Control in Nineteenth Century Britain.* London: Croom Helm.

Douch, R. (1965) Local history in school, *Amateur Historian,* 6(7): 218–22.

Drake, M. (ed.) (1973) *Applied Historical Studies: An Introductory Reader.* London: Methuen.

Durkheim, E. (1904) *The Evolution of Educational Thought.* London: Routledge and Kegan Paul (1977 edn).

Dyhouse, C. (1981) *Girls Growing up in Late Victorian and Edwardian England.* London: Routledge.

Eichelberger, R. (1989) *Disciplined Enquiry: Understanding and Doing Educational Research.* London: Longman.

Elton, G. (1967) *The Practice of History.* Sydney: Sydney University Press.

Elton, G. (1991) *Return to Essentials: Some Reflections on the Present State of Historical Study.* Cambridge: Cambridge University Press.

Erben, M. (1996) The purposes and processes of biographical method, in Scott and Usher (eds) *op. cit.*, pp. 159–74.

Erben, M. (ed.) (1998) *Biography and Education: A Reader*. London: Falmer.

Evans, B. and Waites, B. (1981) *IQ and Mental Testing: An Unnatural Science and its Social History*. London: Macmillan.

Evans, R. J. (1997) *In Defence of History*. London: Granta.

Finkelstein, B. (1989) *Governing the Young: Teacher Behaviour in Popular Primary Schools in Nineteenth Century United States*. London: Falmer.

Finkelstein, B. (1992a) Redoing urban educational history, in Goodenow and Marsden (eds) *op. cit.*, pp. 172–92.

Finkelstein, B. (1992b) Educational historians as mythmakers, in G. Grant (ed.) *Review of Research in Education 18*. Washington, DC: American Educational Research Association, pp. 255–97.

Finkelstein, B. (1998) Classroom management in the United States, 1790–1990: evolving terrain of teaching, in N. B. Shimahara (ed.) *Politics of Classroom Life: Classroom Management in International Perspective*. New York: Garland, pp. 11–48.

Flett, K. (1989) Sex or class: the education of working-class women, 1800–1870, *History of Education*, 18(2): 145–62.

Floud, J. (1954) The educational experience of the adult population of England and Wales as at July 1949, in Glass (ed), *op. cit.*, pp. 98–140.

Forbes, D. (1952) *The Liberal Anglican Idea of History*. Cambridge: Cambridge University Press.

Foster, S. (1999) The struggle for American identity: treatment of ethnic groups in United States history textbooks, *History of Education*, 28(3): 251–78.

Foucault, M. (1977) *Discipline and Punish: The Birth of the Prison*. London: Allen Lane.

Fraenkel, J. and Wallen, N. (1990) *How to Design and Evaluate Research in Education*. New York: McGraw-Hill (3rd edn 1996).

Friar, S. (1991) *The Batsford Companion to Local History*. London: Batsford.

Fussner, F. S. (1962) *The Historical Revolution: English Historical Writing and Thought 1580–1640*. London: Routledge and Kegan Paul.

Gardiner, J. (1988) *What Is History Today . . .?* London: Macmillan.

Gardner, P. (1996) The giant at the front: young teachers and corporal punishment in inter-war elementary schools, *History of Education*, 25(2): 141–63.

Gardner, P. and Cunningham, P. (1997) Oral history and teachers' professional practice: a wartime turning point?, *Cambridge Journal of Education*, 27(3): 331–42.

Glass, D. V. (ed.) (1954) *Social Mobility in Britain*. London: Routledge and Kegan Paul.

Goldthorpe, J. (1991) The uses of history in sociology: reflections on some recent tendencies, *British Journal of Sociology*, 42(2): 211–30.

Good, C. V. (1959) *Introduction to Educational Research*. New York: Appleton-Century-Crofts.

Good, C. V., Barr, A. S. and Scates, D. E. (1936) *The Methodology of Educational Research*. New York: Appleton-Century-Crofts.

Good, C. V. and Scates, D. (1954) *Methods of Research: Educational, Psychological, Sociological*. New York: Appleton-Century-Crofts.

Goodenow, R. and Marsden, W. E. (eds) (1992) *The City and Education in Four Nations*. Cambridge: Cambridge University Press.

Goodenow, R. and Ravitch, D. (eds) (1983) *Schools in Cities: Consensus and Conflict in American Educational History*. London: Holmes and Meier.

Goodson, I. F. (1985) History, context and qualitative methods in the study of curriculum, in Burgess (ed.) *op. cit.*, pp. 121–51.

Goodson, I. F. (1988) *The Making of Curriculum: Collected Essays*. London: Falmer.

Goodson, I. F. (1994) *Studying Curriculum: Cases and Methods*. Buckingham: Open University Press.

Goodson, I. F. (1995) Basil Bernstein and aspects of the sociology of the curriculum, in Atkinson *et al.* (eds) *op. cit.*, pp. 121–36.

Gordon, P. (1983) The writings of Edmond Holmes: a reassessment and bibliography, *History of Education*, 12(1): 15–24.

Gordon, P. (1990) The university professor of education, in J. B. Thomas (ed.) *British Universities and Teacher Education: A Century of Change*. London: Falmer, pp. 163–79.

Gordon, P. (ed.) (1996) *A Guide to Educational Research*. London: Woburn.

Gordon, P. and Aldrich, R. (eds) (1997) *Biographical Dictionary of North American and European Educationists*. London: Woburn.

Gordon, P. and Szreter, R. (eds) (1989) *History of Education: The Making of a Discipline*. London: Woburn.

Gorst, A. and Brivati, B. (1997) The internet for historians, in Butler and Gorst (eds) *op. cit*, pp. 139–53.

Gosden, P. (1976) *Education in the Second World War: A Study in Policy and Administration*. London: Methuen.

Gosden, P. (1981) Twentieth century archives of education as sources for the study of education policy and administration, *Archives*, 15(66): 86–95.

Gosden, P. and Sharp, P. (1978) *The Development of an Education Service: The West Riding 1889 to 1974*. Oxford: Martin Robertson.

Grace, G. (1978) *Teachers, Ideology and Control: A Study in Urban Education*. London: Routledge and Kegan Paul.

Grace, G. (1987) Teachers and the State in Britain: a changing relation, in Lawn and Grace (eds) *op. cit.*, pp. 193–228.

Grace, G. (1991) Welfare Labourism versus the New Right: the struggle in New Zealand's education policy, *International Studies in Sociology of Education*, 1: 25–42.

Grace, G. (1995) Theorising social relations within urban schooling: a sociohistorical analysis, in Atkinson *et al.* (eds), *op. cit.*, pp. 209–27.

Gransden, A. (1982) *Historical Writing in England II: c. 1307 to the Early Sixteenth Century*. London: Routledge and Kegan Paul.

Green, A. (1989) *Education and State Formation: The Rise of Education Systems in England, France and the USA*. New York: St Martin's Press.

Green, A. (1994) Postmodernism and state education, *Journal of Education Policy*, 9(1): 67–83.

Green, A. (1997) *Education, Globalisation and the Nation State*. London: Macmillan.

Grenfell, M. and James, D. (1998) *Bourdieu and Education: Acts of Practical Theory*. London: Falmer.

Griggs, C. (1983) *The Trades Union Congress and the Struggle for Education 1868–1925*. London: Falmer.

Grosvenor, I. (1999) 'There's no place like home': education and the making of national identity, *History of Education*, 28(3): 235–50.

Halpin, D. and Troyna, B. (eds) (1994) *Researching Education Policy: Ethical and Methodological Issues*. London: Falmer.

Halsey, A. H. (1978) *Change in British Society*. Oxford: Oxford University Press.

Halsey, A. H. and Gardner, L. (1953) Selection for secondary education and achievement in four grammar schools, *British Journal of Sociology*, 4: 60–75.

Halsey, A. H., Heath, A. F. and Ridge, J. M. (1980) *Origins and Destinations: Family, Class, and Education in Modern Britain*. Oxford: Clarendon Press.

Hamilton, D. (1989) *Towards a Theory of Schooling*. London: Falmer.

Hargreaves, A. (1994) *Changing Teachers, Changing Times: Teachers' Work and Culture in the Postmodern Age*. London: Cassell.

Hargreaves, D. (1967) *Social Relations in a Secondary School*. London: Routledge and Kegan Paul.

Harrigan, P. J. (1976) The social origins, ambitions, and occupations of secondary students in France during the Second Empire, in Stone (ed.) *op. cit.*, pp. 206–35.

Hay, D. (1977) *Annalists and Historians: Western Historiography from the Eighth to the Eighteenth Centuries*. London: Methuen.

Heath, S. B. (1997) Child's play or finding the ephemera of home, in Hilton *et al.* (eds) *op. cit.*, pp. 17–30.

Hendrick, H. (1990) *Images of Youth: Age, Class, and the Male Youth Problem, 1880–1920*. Oxford: Clarendon Press.

Herber, M. (1997) *Ancestral Trails: The Complete Guide to British Genealogy and Family History*. Stroud: Sutton Publishing.

Hertzberg, H. W. (1980) The teaching of history, in Kammen (ed.), *op. cit.*, pp. 474–504.

Heward, C. (1988) *Making a Man of Him: Parents and Their Sons' Education at an English Public School 1929–1950*. London: Routledge.

Hexter, J. H. (1961) *Reappraisals in History*. London: Longman.

Hey, D. (1998) *Oxford Companion to Local and Family History*. Oxford: Oxford University Press.

Hilton, M. (1997) Introduction, in Hilton *et al.* (eds) *op. cit.*, pp. 1–13.

Hilton, M., Styles, M. and Watson, V. (eds) (1997) *Opening the Nursery Door: Reading, Writing and Childhood 1600–1900*. London: Routledge.

Himmelweit, H. T. (1954) Social status and secondary education since the 1944 Act: some data for London, in Glass (ed.) *op. cit.*, pp. 141–59.

History of Education Quarterly (1989) Forum: The metropolitan experience in American education, 29(3): 419–46.

Hitchcock, G. and Hughes, D. (1989) *Research and the Teacher: a Qualitative Introduction to School-based Research*. London: Routledge (2nd edn 1995).

Hobsbawm, E. and Ranger, T. (eds) (1983) *The Invention of Tradition*. Cambridge: Cambridge University Press.

Hofstadter, R. (1968) History and sociology in the United States, in S. Lipset and R. Hofstadter (eds) *Sociology and History: Methods*. New York: Basic Books, pp. 3–19.

Honey, J. R. de S. (1977) *Tom Brown's Universe: The Development of the English Public School in the Nineteenth Century*. London: Millington.

Hoskin, K. (1979) The examination, disciplinary power and rational schooling, *History of Education*, 8(2): 135–46.

Hoskin, K. (1982) Examinations and the schooling of science, in R. MacLeod (ed.) *Days of Judgement: Science, Examinations and the Organisation of Knowledge in Late Victorian England*. Driffield: Nafferton Books.

Hoskin, K. (1990) Foucault under examination: the crypto-educationalist unmasked, in Ball (ed.) *op. cit.*, pp. 29–53.

Howard, M. (1991) *The Lessons of History*. Oxford: Oxford University Press.

Howarth, K. (1998) *Oral History: A Handbook*. Stroud: Sutton Publishing.

Hughes, T. (1857) *Tom Brown's Schooldays*, ed. A. Sanders. Oxford: Oxford University Press (1989 edn).

Humphries, S. (1981) *Hooligans or Rebels? An Oral History of Working Class Childhood and Youth*. Oxford: Blackwell.

Huppert, G. (1997) The Annales experiment, in M. Bentley (ed.) *Companion to Historiography*. London: Routledge.

Jaeger, R. M. (ed.) (1988) *Complementary Methods for Research in Education*. Washington, DC: American Educational Research Association.

Jefferys, K. (1984) R. A. Butler, the Board of Education and the 1944 Education Act, *History*, 227: 415–31.

Jenkins, K. (1995) *On 'What is History?': from Carr and Elton to Rorty and White*. London: Routledge.

Johnson, R. (1970) Educational policy and social control in early Victorian England, *Past and Present*, 49: 96–119.

Johnson, R. (1989) Thatcherism and English education: breaking the mould or confirming the pattern? *History of Education*, 18(2): 91–121.

Kaestle, C. (1976) 'Between the Scylla of brutal ignorance and the Charybdis of a literary education': elite attitudes toward mass schooling in early industrial England and America, in Stone (ed.) *op. cit.*, pp. 177–91.

Kaestle, C. (1988) Recent methodological developments in the history of American education, in Jaeger (ed.), *op. cit.*, pp. 61–71, 79–80.

Kaestle, C. (1990) Introduction to special issue on the history of literacy, *History of Education Quarterly*, 30(4): 487–91.

Kaestle, C., Dama-Moore, H., Stedman, L., Tinsley, K. and Trollinger, W. (1991) *Literacy in the United States: Readers and Reading since 1880*. New Haven, CT: Yale University Press.

Kamm, J. (1965) *Hope Deferred: Girls' Education in English History*. London: Methuen.

Kammen, M. (ed.) (1980) *The Past Before Us: Contemporary Historical Writing in the United States*. Ithaca, NY: Cornell University Press.

Karabel, J. and Halsey, A. H. (1977) Educational research: a review and an interpretation, in J. Karabel and A. H. Halsey (eds) *Power and Ideology in Education*. New York: Oxford University Press, pp. 1–85.

Katz, M. B. (1968) *The Irony of Early School Reform*. Cambridge, MA: Harvard University Press.

Keeves, J. (ed.) (1988) *Educational Research, Methodology and Measurement: An International Handbook*. Oxford: Pergamon Press (2nd edn 1997).

Kenyon, J. (1983) *The History Men: The Historical Profession in England since the Renaissance*. London: Weidenfeld and Nicolson.

Kerckhoff, A., Fogelman, K., Crook, D. and Reeder, D. (1996) *Going Comprehensive in England and Wales: A Study of Uneven Change*. London: Woburn.

Kirk, D. and Twigg, K. (1994) Regulating Australian bodies: eugenics, anthropometrics and school medical inspection in Victoria, 1900–1940, *History of Education Review*, 23(1): 19–37.

Kliebard, H. (1990) Curriculum policy as symbolic action: connecting education with the workplace, in H. Haft and S. Hopmann (eds) *Case Studies in Curriculum Administration History*. London: Falmer, pp. 143–58.

Kliebard, H. (1996) Constructing the concept of curriculum on the Wisconsin frontier: how school restructuring sustained a pedagogical revolution, *History of Education*, 25(2): 123–39.

Kridel, C. (ed.) (1998) *Writing Educational Biography: Explorations in Qualitative Research*. London: Garland.

Labaree, D. (1988) *The Making of an American High School: The Credentials Market and the Central High School of Philadelphia, 1838–1939*. New Haven, CT: Yale University Press.

Lacey, C. (1970) *Hightown Grammar: The School as a Social System*. Manchester: Manchester University Press.

Lagemann, E. (1997) Contested terrain: a history of education research in the United States, 1890–1990, *Educational Researcher*, 26(9): 5–17.

Laslett, P. (1965) *The World We Have Lost*. London: Methuen (3rd edn 1983).

Lawn, M. (1996) *Modern Times? Work, Professionalism and Citizenship in Teaching*. London: Falmer.

Lawn, M. and Grace, G. (eds) (1987) *Teachers: The Culture and Politics of Work*. London: Falmer.

Lawson, J. and Silver, H. (1973) *A Social History of Education in England*. London: Methuen.

Layton, D. (1984) *Interpreters of Science: A History of the Association for Science Education*. London: John Murray/ASE.

Leach, A. F. (1896) *English Schools at the Reformation, 1646–8*. London: Constable.

Leach, A. F. (1911) *Educational Charters and Documents 598 to 1909*. Cambridge: Cambridge University Press.

Le Goff, J. (1983) Past and Present: later history, *Past and Present*, 100: 14–28.

Leinster-Mackay, D. with Sarfaty, E. (1994) *Education and The Times: An Index of Letters to 1910*. London: Mansell.

Lingard, B. and Douglas, P. (1999) *Men Engaging Feminisms: Pro-feminism Backlashes and Schooling*. Buckingham: Open University Press.

Lowe, R. (1983) History as propaganda: the strange uses of the history of education, in R. Lowe (ed.), *Trends in the Study and Teaching of the History of Education*. Leicester: History of Education Society, pp. 48–60.

Lundgreen, P. (1976) Educational expansion and economic growth in nineteenth century Germany: a quantitative study, in Stone (ed.), *op. cit.*, pp. 20–66.

McCann, P. (ed.) (1977) *Popular Education and Socialisation in the Nineteenth Century*. London: Methuen.

McCulloch, G. (1986) *Education in the Forming of New Zealand Society: Needs and Opportunities for Study*. Wellington: New Zealand Association for Educational Research.

McCulloch, G. (1988) Imperial and colonial designs: the case of Auckland Grammar School, *History of Education*, 17(4): 257–67.

McCulloch, G. (1989) *The Secondary Technical School: A Usable Past?* London: Falmer.

McCulloch, G. (1991) School zoning, equity and freedom: the case of New Zealand, *Journal of Education Policy*, 6(2): 155–68.

McCulloch, G. (1994) *Educational Reconstruction: The 1944 Education Act and the Twenty-first Century*. London: Woburn.

McCulloch, G. (1995) The power of three: 'parity of esteem' and the social history of tripartism, in E. W. Jenkins (ed.) *Studies in the History of Education*. Leeds: Leeds University Press, pp. 114–32.

McCulloch, G. (1996) Educating the public: Tawney, the *Manchester Guardian* and educational reform, in Aldrich (ed.) *op. cit.*, pp. 116–37.

McCulloch, G. (1998) *Failing the Ordinary Child? The Theory and Practice of Working Class Secondary Education*. Buckingham: Open University Press.

McCulloch, G., Helsby, G. and Knight, P. (2000) *The Politics of Professionalism: Teachers and the Curriculum*. London: Continuum.

Mack, E. C. (1938) *Public Schools and British Opinion 1780 to 1860*. London: Methuen.

Mack, E. C. (1941) *Public Schools and British Opinion since 1860*. London: Methuen.

MacLeod, A. S. (1975) *A Moral Tale: Children's Fiction and American Culture, 1820–1860*. Handen, CT: Archer.

MacLeod, A. S. (1976) Education for freedom: children's fiction in Jacksonian America, *Harvard Educational Review*, 46(3): 425–35.

Maclure, J. S. (1965) *Educational Documents: England and Wales 1816–1967*. London: Methuen.

Maclure, J. S. (1984) *Educational Development and School Building: Aspects of Public Policy 1945 to 1973*. London: Longman.

McMahon, J. (1996) ANZHES: the first twenty-five years, *History of Education Review*, 25(1): 1–22.

Mangan, J. A. (1986) *Athleticism in the Victorian and Edwardian Public School*. London: Falmer.

Mangan, J. A. and Walvin, J. (eds) (1987) *Manliness and Morality: Middle-class Masculinity in Britain and America, 1800–1940*. Manchester: Manchester University Press.

Marginson, S. (1997) *Markets in Education*. Sydney: Allen & Unwin.

Marker, M. (1999) 'That history is more a part of the present than it ever was in the past': toward an ethnohistory of native education, *History of Education Review*, 28(1): 17–29.

Marker, M. (2000) Ethnohistory and indigenous education: a moment of uncertainty *History of Education*, 29(1): 79–85.

Marsden, W. E. (1979) Census enumerators' returns, schooling and social areas in the late Victorian town: a case study of Bootle, in R. Lowe (ed.) *New Approaches to the Study of Popular Education, 1851–1902*. Leicester: History of Education Society, pp. 16–35.

Marsden, W. E. (1987) *Unequal Educational Provision in England and Wales: The Nineteenth Century Roots*. London: Woburn.

Marsden, W. E. (1990) Rooting racism into the educational experience of childhood and youth in the nineteenth and twentieth centuries, *History of Education*, 19(4): 333–53.

Marsden, W. E. (1992) Social stratification and nineteenth century English urban education, in Goodenow and Marsden (eds) *op. cit.*, pp. 111–28.

Martin, J. (1999) *Women and the Politics of Schooling in Victorian and Edwardian England*. Leicester: Leicester University Press.

Mayeur, F. (1984) Recent work in the history of education in France, *European History Quarterly*, 14(1): 93–102.

Meyer, J., Kamens, D. and Benavot, A. (1992) *School Knowledge for the Masses: World Models and National Primary Curricular Categories in the Twentieth Century*. London: Falmer.

Meyers, P. (1994) Education, in P. Stearns (ed.) *op. cit.*, pp. 221–5.

Mills, C. W. (1959) *The Sociological Imagination*. New York: Oxford University Press.

Ministry of Education (1959) *15 to 18* (Crowther Report). London: HMSO.

Mitch, D. F. (1992) *The Rise of Popular Literacy in Victorian England: The Influence of Private Choice and Public Policy*. Philadelphia: University of Pennsylvania Press.

Mitchell, S. (ed.) (1998) *Victorian Britain: An Encyclopedia*. London: St James Press.

Morton, A. (1997) *Education and the State from 1833*. PRO Readers' Guide no. 18. London: PRO Publications.

Moss, M. (1997) Archives, the historian and the future, in Bentley (ed.) *op. cit.*, pp. 960–73.

Motley, M. (1994) Educating the English gentleman abroad: the Verney family in seventeenth-century France and Holland, *History of Education*, 23(3): 243–56.

Muller, D., Ringer, F. and Simon, B. (eds) (1987) *The Rise of the Modern Educational System: Structural Change and Social Reproduction 1870–1920*. Cambridge: Cambridge University Press.

Musgrave, P. W. (ed.) (1970) *Sociology, History and Education: A Reader*. London: Methuen.

Newsom, J. H. (1948) *The Education of Girls*. London: Faber.

Nolan, M. (2000) Putting the state in its place: the domestic education debate in New Zealand, *History of Education*, 29(6).

Norwood, C. (1929) *The English Tradition of Education*. London: John Murray.

Ollerenshaw, K. (1961) *Education for Girls*. London: Faber.

Openshaw, R., Lee, G. and Lee, H. (1993) *Challenging the Myths: Rethinking New Zealand's Educational History*. Palmerston North: The Dunmore Press.

Opie, I. and Opie, P. (1951) *The Oxford Dictionary of Nursery Rhymes*. Oxford: Oxford University Press.

Opie, I. and Opie, P. (1959) *The Lore and Language of School Children*. Oxford: Oxford University Press.

Opie, I. and Opie, P. (1969) *Children's Games in Street and Playground*. Oxford: Oxford University Press.

Orme, N. (1973) *English Schools in the Middle Ages*. London: Methuen.

Orme, N. (1984) *From Childhood to Chivalry: the Education of the English Kings and Aristocracy, 1066–1531*. London: Methuen.

Orme, N. (1989) *Education and Society in Medieval England*. London: Hambledon Press.

Ozga, J. (ed.) (1988) *Schoolwork: Approaches to the Labour Process of Teaching*. Milton Keynes: Open University Press.

Ozga, J. and Gewirtz, S. (1994) Sex, lies and audiotape: interviewing the education policy elite, in D. Halpin and B. Troyna (eds) *Researching Education Policy: Ethical and Methodological Issues*. London: Falmer Press, pp. 212–35.

Parker, C. (1990) *The English Historical Tradition since 1850*. Edinburgh: John Donald.

Percy, E. (1958) *Some Memories*. London: Eyre and Spottiswoode.

Perks, R. (1990) *Oral History: an Annotated Bibliography*. London: The British Library.

Petersen, R. C. (1992) *History of Education Research: What It Is and How to Do It*. Sydney: NTU Services.

Phelps, P., Jones, M. and Jones, G. (1974–75) A curricular experiment, *Local Historian*, 11: 331–5.

Platt, J. (1981) Evidence and proof in documentary research, *Sociological Review*, 29(1): 31–66.

Plumb, J. H. (1982) Editorial foreword to the Pelican Social History of Britain series.

Pollard, S. (1989) *Britain's Prime and Britain's Decline*. London: Edward Arnold.

Prosser, J. (ed.) (1998) *Image-based Research: A Sourcebook for Qualitative Researchers*. London: Falmer.

Purvis, J. (1983) Towards a history of women's education in nineteenth century Britain: a sociological analysis, in J. Purvis and M. Hales (eds) *Achievement and Inequality in Education*. London: Routledge and Kegan Paul, pp. 153–92.

Purvis, J. (1985) Reflections upon doing historical documentary research from a feminist perspective, in Burgess (ed.) *op. cit.*, pp. 179–205.

Purvis, J. (1989a) 'We can no longer pretend that sex stratification does not exist, nor that it exists but is unimportant' (M. Eichler). A reply to Keith Flett, *History of Education*, 18(2): 147–52.

Purvis, J. (1989b) *Hard Lessons: The Lives and Education of Working-class Women in Nineteenth-century England*. Cambridge: Polity Press.

Purvis, J. (1991) *A History of Women's Education in England*. Buckingham: Open University Press.

Purvis, J. (1992) The historiography of British education: a feminist critique, in A. Rattansi and D. Reeder (eds) *Rethinking Radical Education*. London: Lawrence and Wishart, pp. 249–66.

Quick, R. H. (1868) *Essays on Educational Reformers*. London: Longman (1895 edn).

Quigly, I. (1982) *The Heirs of Tom Brown: The English School Story*. London: Chatto and Windus.

Rashdall, H. (1895) *The Universities of Europe in the Middle Ages* (2 vols). Oxford: Clarendon Press.

Raven, J. (1989) Viewpoint: British history and the enterprise culture. *Past and Present*, 123: 178–204.

Reeder, D. (ed.) (1979) *Urban Education in the Nineteenth Century*. London: Taylor and Francis.

Reese, W. J. (1998) American high school political economy in the nineteenth century, *History of Education*, 27(3): 255–66.

Reid, W. A. (1990) Strange curricula: origins and development of the institutional categories of schooling, *Journal of Curriculum Studies*, 22(3): 203–16.

Richardson, W. (1999a) Historians and educationists: the history of education as a field of study in post-war England, Part I: 1945–72, *History of Education*, 28(1): 1–30.

Richardson, W. (1999b) Historians and educationists: the history of education as a field of study in post-war England. Part II: 1972–96, *History of Education*, 28(2): 109–41.

Richardson, W. (2000) History, education and audience, in D. Crook and R. Aldrich (eds) *History of Education for the Twenty-first Century*. London: Institute of Education.

Ringer, F. (1977) Problems in the history of higher education: a review article, *Comparative Studies in Society and History*, 19: 239–55.

Ringer, F. (1979) *Education and Society in Modern Europe*. London: Indiana University Press.

Ringer, F. (1987) Introduction, in Muller *et al.* (eds) *op. cit.*, pp. 1–12.

Roach, J. (1971) *Public Examinations in England, 1850–1900*. Cambridge: Cambridge University Press.

Roach, J. (1986) *A History of Secondary Education in England, 1800–1870*. London: Longman.

Roach, J. (1991) *Secondary Education in England 1870–1902: Public Activity and Private Enterprise*. London: Routledge.

Rose, J. (1993) Willingly to school: the working class response to elementary education in Britain, 1875–1918, *Journal of British Studies*, 32(2): 114–38.

Rousmaniere, K. (1997) *City Teachers: Teaching and School Reform in Historical Perspective*. New York: Teachers College Press.

Rousmaniere, K., Dehli, K. and de Coninck-Smith, N. (1997) Moral regulation and schooling: an introduction, in K. Rousmaniere, K. Dehli and N. de Coninck-Smith (eds) *Discipline, Moral Regulation, and Schooling: A Social History*. London: Garland, pp. 3–17.

Rousmaniere, K., Lawn, M. and Grosvenor, I. (eds) (1999) *Silences and Images: The Social History of the Classroom*. London: Peter Lang.

Royal Commission on Secondary Education (1895) *Report of the Commissioners* (Bryce Report). London: HMSO.

Rubinstein, W. D. (1993) *Capitalism, Culture, and Decline in Britain 1750–1990*. London: Routledge.

Sanderson, M. (1994) *The Missing Stratum: Technical School Education 1900 to 1990s*. London: Athlone Press.

Sanderson, M. (1999) *Education and Economic Decline in Britain, 1870 to the 1990s*. Cambridge: Cambridge University Press and Economic History Society.

Saran, R. (1985) The use of archives and interviews in research on educational policy, in Burgess (ed.) *op. cit.*, pp. 207–41.

Saul, N. (1983) *The Batsford Companion to Medieval England*. London: Batsford.

Schools Council (1967) *A School Approach to Technology* (Curriculum Bulletin no. 2). London: Schools Council.

Scott, D. and Usher, R. (eds) (1996) *Understanding Educational Research*. London: Routledge.

Scott, D. and Usher, R. (1999) *Researching Education: Data, Methods and Theory in Educational Enquiry*. London: Cassell.

Scott, J. (1990) *A Matter of Record: Documentary Sources in Social Research*. Cambridge: Polity Press.

Seaborne, M. (1971) *The English School: Its Architecture and Organisation. Vol. I: 1370–1870*. London: Routledge and Kegan Paul.

Seaborne, M. and Lowe, R. (1977) *The English School: Its Architecture and Organisation. Vol. II: 1870–1970.* London: Routledge and Kegan Paul.

Selleck, R. J. W. (1991) Review essay, *History of Education Review*, 20(2): 92–3.

Selleck, R. J. W. (1994) *James Kay-Shuttleworth: Journey of an Outsider.* London: Woburn.

Silver, H. (1973) Introduction, in H. Silver (ed.) *Equal Opportunity in Education: a Reader in Social Class and Educational Opportunity.* London: Methuen, pp. xi–xxxiv.

Silver, H. (1980) Nothing but the present, or nothing but the past? in P. Gordon (ed.) *The Study of Education: Inaugural Lectures.* London: Woburn, pp. 265–84.

Silver, H. (1981) Policy as history and as theory, *British Journal of Sociology of Education*, 2(3): 293–9.

Silver, H. (1983) *Education as History: Interpreting Nineteenth- and Twentieth-century Education.* London: Methuen.

Silver, H. (1990) *Education, Change and the Policy Process.* London: Falmer.

Simon, B. (1960) *The Two Nations and the Educational Structure, 1780–1870.* London: Lawrence and Wishart.

Simon, B. (1965) *Education and the Labour Movement, 1870–1920.* London: Lawrence and Wishart.

Simon, B. (1966) The history of education, in J. W. Tibble (ed.) *The Study of Education.* London: Routledge and Kegan Paul, pp. 91–131.

Simon, B. (1974) *The Politics of Educational Reform, 1920–1940.* London: Lawrence and Wishart.

Simon, B. (1986) The 1944 Education Act: a Conservative measure? *History of Education*, 15(1): 31–43.

Simon, B. (1990) The study of education as a university subject, in J. Thomas (ed.) *British Universities and Teacher Education: A Century of Change.* London: Falmer.

Simon, B. (1991) *Education and the Social Order, 1940–1990.* London: Lawrence and Wishart.

Simon, B. (1998) *A Life in Education.* London: Lawrence and Wishart.

Simon, J. (1989) Promoting educational reform on the home front: The TES and The Times, 1940–1944, *History of Education*, 18(3): 195–212.

Simpson, J. H. (1923) *The Public Schools and Athleticism.* London: Educational Times Booklets.

Skager, R. and Weinberg, C. (1971) *Fundamentals of Educational Research.* Glenver, IL: Scott Foreman and Co.

Skipp, V. H. T. (1967) The use of local history in the schools, in Finberg (ed.) *op. cit.*, pp. 103–27.

Slavin, R. (1984) *Research Methods in Education: A Practical Guide.* Englewood Cliffs, NJ: Prentice Hall.

Slee, P. R. H. (1986) *Learning and a Liberal Education: The Study of Modern History in the Universities of Oxford, Cambridge and Manchester, 1800–1914.* Manchester: Manchester University Press.

Slee, P. R. H. (1988) Profession of history, in Cannon *et al.* (eds) *op. cit.*, pp. 343–4.

Smeaton, R. F. (1999) *Researching Education: Reference Tools and Networks.* Hull: LISE.

Smelser, N. (1991) *Social Paralysis and Social Change: British Working-class Education in the Nineteenth Century*. Berkeley: University of California Press.

Smith, A. (1997) The English-language historiography of Modern Japan, in Bentley (ed.) *op. cit.*, pp. 659–76.

Smith, H. B. (1927) *The Nation's Schools: Their Task and Their Importance*. London: Longman.

Smith, J. T. (1998) *Punch* and elementary education (1860–1900). *History of Education*, 27(2): 125–40.

Smith, L., Dwyer, D., Prunty, J. and Kleine, P. (1988) *Innovation and Change in Schooling: History, Politics, and Agency*. London: Falmer.

Soffer, R. (1994) *Discipline and Power: The University, History, and the Making of an English Elite, 1870–1930*. Stanford, CA: Stanford University Press.

Spaull, A. D. (1981) The biographical tradition in the history of Australian education, *ANZHES Journal*, 10(2): 1–10.

Spaull, A. D. (1988) Oral history, in J. P. Keeves (ed.) *Educational Research Methodology and Measurement: An International Handbook*. Oxford: Pergamon Press.

Spencer, F. H. (1938) *An Inspector's Testament*. London: English Universities Press.

Spolton, L. (1962) The secondary school in post-war fiction, *British Journal of Educational Studies*, 9: 124–41.

Springhall, J. (1986) *Coming of Age: Adolescence in Britain 1860–1960*. Dublin: Gill and Macmillan.

Springhall, J. (1987) Building character in the British boy: the attempt to extend Christian manliness to working class adolescents, 1880–1914, in Mangan and Walvin (eds) *op. cit.*, pp. 52–74.

Springhall, J. (1998) *Youth, Popular Culture and Moral Panics: Penny Gaffs to Gangsta-rap, 1830–1996*. London: Macmillan.

Stearns, P. N. (1980) Toward a wider vision: trends in social history, in Kammen (ed.) *op. cit.*, pp. 205–30.

Stearns, P. N. (ed.) (1994) *Encyclopedia of Social History*. New York: Garland.

Stedman Jones, G. (1976) From historical sociology to theoretical history, *British Journal of Sociology*, 27(3): 295–305.

Stedman Jones, G. (1982) *Languages of Class: Studies in English Working Class History, 1832–1982*. Cambridge: Cambridge University Press.

Steedman, C. (1985) The mother made conscious: the historical development of a primary school pedagogy, *History Workshop Journal*, 20: 149–63.

Stephens, W. B. (1973) *Regional Variations in Education During the Industrial Revolution, 1780–1870: The Task of the Local Historian*. Leeds: University of Leeds.

Stephens, W. B. (1981) *Sources for English Local History*. Cambridge: Cambridge University Press.

Stephens, W. B. (1987) *Education, Literacy and Society, 1830–70: the Geography of Diversity in Provincial England*. Manchester: Manchester University Press.

Stephens, W. B. (1999) *Education in Britain 1750–1914*. London: Macmillan.

Stevenson, D. (1993) The end of history? The British university experience, 1981–92, *Contemporary Record*, 7(1): 66–85.

Stone, L. (1964) The educational revolution in England, 1560–1640, *Past and Present*, 28: 41–80.

Stone, L. (1969) Literacy and education in England, 1640–1900, *Past and Present*, 42: 69–139.

Stone, L. (ed.) (1974) *The University in Society*. Princeton, NJ: Princeton University Press.

Stone, L. (ed.) (1976) *Schooling and Society: Studies in the History of Education*. Baltimore: Johns Hopkins University Press.

Stray, C. (1994) Paradigms regained: towards a historical sociology of the textbook, *Journal of Curriculum Studies*, 26(1): 1–29.

Strayer, J. (1982–89) *Dictionary of the Middle Ages* (13 vols). New York: Charles Scribner's Sons.

Sutherland, G. (1969) *Elementary Education in the Nineteenth Century*. London: Historical Association.

Sutherland, G. (1981) A view of education records in the nineteenth and twentieth centuries, *Archives*, 15(66): 79–85.

Sutherland, G. (1984) *Ability, Merit and Measurement: Mental Testing and English Education 1880–1940*. Oxford: Clarendon Press.

Sutherland, N. and Barman, J. (1992) Out of the shadows: retrieving the history of urban education and urban childhood in Canada, in Goodenow and Marsden (eds) *op. cit.*, pp. 87–108.

Swindells, J. (ed.) (1995) *The Uses of Autobiography*. London: Taylor and Francis.

Sylvester, D. W. (ed.) (1970) *Educational Documents 800–1816*. London: Methuen.

Szarmach, P., Tavormina, M. and Rosenthal, J. (eds) (1998) *Medieval England: An Encyclopedia*. New York: Garland.

Szreter, R. (1969) History and sociology: rivals or partners in the field of education?, *History of Education Society Bulletin*, 3: 17–24.

Szreter, S. (1997) British economic decline and human resources, in P. Clarke and C. Trebilcock (eds) *Understanding Decline: Perceptions and Realities of British Economic Performance*. Cambridge: Cambridge University Press, pp. 73–102.

Taylor, W. (1996) Education and the Moot, in R. Aldrich (ed.) *In History and in Education*. London: Woburn, pp. 159–86.

Teese, R. (1995) Scholastic power and curriculum access: public and private schooling in postwar Australia, *History of Education*, 24(4): 353–67.

Thatcher, M. (1995) *The Path to Power*. London: HarperCollins.

Theobald, M. (1996) *Knowing Women: Origins of Women's Education in Nineteenth Century Australia*. Cambridge: Cambridge University Press.

Theobald, M. (2000) Women, leadership and gender politics in the interwar years: the case of Julia Flynn, *History of Education*, 29(1): 63–77.

Thomas, K. (1976) *Rule and Misrule in the Schools of Early Modern England* (The Stenton Lecture 1975). Reading: University of Reading.

Thomas, K. (1986) The meaning of literacy in early modern England, in G. Baumann (ed.) *The Written Word: Literacy in Transition*. Oxford: Clarendon.

Thomas, K. (1987) Numeracy in early modern England, *Transactions of the Royal Historical Society* (5th series), 37: 103–32.

Thompson, P. (1988) *The Voice of the Past: Oral History*. Oxford: Oxford University Press.

Tilly, C. (1981) *As Sociology Meets History*. London: Academic Press.

Times Educational Supplement (1960) Leading article: dodging the issue. *TES*, 25 March.

Timutimu, N., Simon, J. and Matthews, K. (1998) Historical research as a bicultural project: seeking new perspectives on the New Zealand Native Schools system, *History of Education*, 27(2): 109–24.

Tosh, J. (1999) *A Man's Place: Masculinity and the Middle-class Home in Victorian England*. London: Yale University Press.

Tosh, J. (2000 [1984]) *The Pursuit of History*, revised edn. London: Longman.

Turney, B. and Robb, G. (1971) *Research in Education: An Introduction*. Hinsdale, IL: The Dryden Press.

Tyack, D. and Cuban, L. (1995) *Tinkering Toward Utopia: A Century of Public School Reform*. Cambridge, MA: Harvard University Press.

Unwin, R. (1983) Visual sources and the history of education, *History of Education Society Bulletin*, 31: 24–48.

Usher, R. and Edwards, R. (1994) *Postmodernism and Education*. London: Routledge.

Van Dalen, D. (1962) *Understanding Educational Research*. New York: McGraw-Hill.

Verma, G. and Beard, R. (1981) *What Is Educational Research? Perspectives on Techniques of Research*. Aldershot: Gower.

Verma, G. K. and Mallick, K. (eds) (1999) *Researching Education: Perspectives and Techniques*. London: Falmer.

Vincent, D. (1982) *Bread, Knowledge and Freedom: A Study of Nineteenth-century Working Class Autobiography*. London: Methuen.

Vincent, D. (1989) *Literacy and Popular Culture: England 1750–1914*. Cambridge: Cambridge University Press.

Vinovskis, M. (1995) *Education, Society, and Economic Opportunity: A Historical Perspective on Persistent Issues*. London: Yale University Press.

Walford, G. (ed.) (1991) *Doing Educational Research*. London: Routledge and Kegan Paul.

Walford, G. (ed.) (1998) *Doing Research about Education*. London: Falmer.

Walkerdine, V. (1984) Developmental psychology and the child-centred pedagogy: the insertion of Piaget into early education, in J. Henriques *et al.* (eds) *Changing the Subject: Psychology, Social Regulation and Subjectivity*. London: Methuen, pp. 153–202.

Warburton, T. and Saunders, M. (1996) Representing teachers' professional culture through cartoons, *British Journal of Educational Studies*, 44(3): 307–25.

Waring, M. (1979) Background to Nuffield Science, *History of Education*, 8(3): 223–37.

Warwick, D. and Williams, J. (1980) History and the sociology of education, *British Journal of Sociology of Education*, 1(3): 333–46.

Watson, F. (1909) *The Beginnings of the Teaching of Modern Subjects in England*. Merston: Scolar Press (1971 edn).

Weiler, K. and Middleton, S. (eds) (1999) *Telling Women's Lives: Narrative Enquiries in the History of Women's Education*. Buckingham: Open University Press.

Weiner, G. (1994) *Feminisms in Education: An Introduction*. Buckingham: Open University Press.

Wiener, M. (1981) *English Culture and the Decline of the Industrial Spirit 1850–1980*. Cambridge: Cambridge University Press.

Wiersma, W. (1969) *Research Methods in Education: An Introduction.* Itasca, IL: FE Peacock.

Williams, R. (1961) *The Long Revolution.* Harmondsworth: Penguin.

Wilson, J. D. (1984) From social control to family strategies: some observations on recent trends in Canadian educational history, *History of Education Review*, 13(1): 1–13.

Wiseman, D. (1999) *Research Strategies for Education.* Bellmont, CA: Wadsworth Publishing Co.

Woodhead, C. (1998) Review, *New Statesman*, 20 March.

Wooldridge, A. (1995) *Measuring the Mind: Education and Psychology in England, c. 1860–1990.* Cambridge: Cambridge University Press.

Young, R. (1990) *White Mythologies: Writing History and the West.* London: Routledge.

Young, M. (1958) *The Rise of the Meritocracy 1870–2033: An Essay on Education and Equality.* London: Thames and Hudson.

Young, M. F. D. (ed.) (1971) *Knowledge and Control: New Directions for the Sociology of Education.* London: Collier-Macmillan.

Youngman, M. (ed.) (1978) *Historical Research: Rediguide 15.* Maidenhead: TRC-Rediguides.

Index

EDUCATIONAL RESEARCH UNDONE
THE POSTMODERN EMBRACE

Ian Stronach and Maggie MacLure

> As intelligent a hearing as postmodernism is likely to receive.
>
> Professor Ernie House, School of Education, University of
> Colorado at Boulder

> This is a provocative, important book. It moves the discourses of post-modernism and deconstructionism to new levels of insight and analysis. Authors Stronach and MacLure perform a major service to the field, showing how these complex discourses can be fitted to the concrete practices of educational research and pedagogy. In so doing they set new goals and priorities for the next generation of educational research and theory.
>
> Norman K. Denzin, College of Communications Scholar,
> Distinguished Professor of Communication, Research Professor
> of Sociology, Criticism and Interpretive Theory,
> University of Illinois at Urbana-Champaign

This book is the first educational research text in the UK to come to terms with postmodernism and deconstruction, connecting these emerging problematics of 'representation' to issues in philosophy, research methodology, and policy critique, and both providing and criticizing its own examples. The authors draw on literary theory, anthropology and sociology in order to construct alternative ways of reading and writing educational research, claiming that it is with a 'reformed inheritance' that such research can best address the condition of postmodernity as well as the positive and negative aspects of postmodernism. The book will appeal to educational and social researchers, as well as to research students.

Contents

208pp   0 335 19433 8 (paperback)   0 335 19434 6 (hardback)

FAILING THE ORDINARY CHILD?
THE THEORY AND PRACTICE OF WORKING-CLASS SECONDARY EDUCATION

Gary McCulloch

- How have the ideals of working-class secondary education related to its practical outcomes, and to what extent has it failed the 'ordinary child'?
- How can the historical tradition of working-class secondary education illuminate our understanding of contemporary debates at the end of the 20th century?

In seeking to answer these questions, this book explores working-class secondary education over the past century in terms that help to explain the unresolved issues and debates of the 1990s. It focuses on social distinctions in secondary education, and especially on initiatives designed to provide for the mass of the population, or the 'ordinary child'. These inititatives culminated in the secondary modern schools which only a generation ago were the main providers of secondary education in England and Wales. The book discusses general social and historical issues relating to working-class secondary education, and the emergence of the idea in the late nineteenth century. It examines the experiment of the secondary modern schools in detail to appraise the reasons for their rise, their successes and their ultimate failure. It also pursues the underlying theme of differentiation in secondary education since the 1960s, its continuing influence despite the spread of comprehensive schools over that time, and its role in the educational and social debates at the end of the century.

Contents

208pp   0 335 19787 6 (paperback)   0 335 19788 4 (hardback)

TELLING WOMEN'S LIVES
NARRATIVE INQUIRIES IN THE HISTORY OF WOMEN'S EDUCATION

Kathleen Weiler and Sue Middleton (eds)

This collection brings together the work of scholars exploring the history of women in education in a number of different national settings. The contributors include both established scholars who have completed major studies and younger scholars exploring new directions. All of these writers share an engagement in reflection on the process of history writing and consider the impact of recent theoretical debates on their own scholarship. Their work reflects the influence of feminist theory and poststructuralism, but also of postcolonial theory and theories of the educational state. In these essays, writers address such key issues as the nature of historical evidence, the continuing need to uncover the 'hidden histories' of women as teachers, the ways life history narratives can illuminate women's own conceptions of themselves as women and teachers, the material conditions of teaching as work for women, and the way conceptions of gender have shaped women's experiences in relation to the educational state, the family, class, sexuality and race. These feminist writers also explore the ways they are implicated in the very subject of their research – the educated woman who is also an educator.

Contents

176pp   0 335 20173 3 (paperback)   0 335 20174 1 (hardback)